Haynes

Build your own
Computer

2nd Edition

© Haynes Publishing 2005
First published 2003
Reprinted 2004 (twice)

Published by: Haynes Publishing
Sparkford, Yeovil, Somerset BA22 7JJ, UK
Tel: 01963 442030 Fax: 01963 440001
Int. tel: +44 1963 442030 Fax: +44 1963 440001
E-mail: sales@haynes.co.uk
Website: www.haynes.co.uk

British Library Cataloguing in Publication Data:
A catalogue record for this book is available from the British Library

ISBN 1 84425 228 0

Printed in Britain by J. H. Haynes & Co. Ltd., Sparkford

Throughout this book, trademarked names are used. Rather than put a
trademark symbol after every occurrence of a trademarked name, we use
the names in an editorial fashion only, and to the benefit of the trademark
owner, with no intention of infringement of the trademark. Where such
designations appear in this book, they have been printed with initial caps.

Whilst we at J. H. Haynes & Co. Ltd. strive to ensure the accuracy and
completeness of the information in this book, it is provided entirely at the
risk of the user. Neither the company nor the author can accept liability
for any errors, omissions or damage resulting therefrom. In particular,
users should be aware that component and accessory manufacturers, and
software providers, can change specifications without notice, thus
appropriate professional advice should always be sought.

Haynes

Build your own Computer

2nd Edition

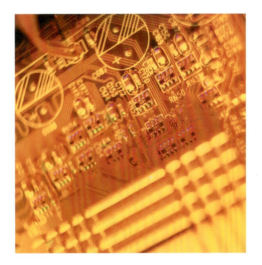

Contents

Introduction

Welcome to this fully updated and revised guide to building your own PC. As ever, technology has moved on apace since the first edition of this book so we've taken this opportunity to introduce the latest processors, memory, interfaces and more. We've also expanded the step-by-step sections to talk you through two complete projects: a standard tower PC and a smart smaller computer designed for gaming or for home entertainment. Between them, they cover pretty much everything you need to know.

As always in Haynes computer books, we focus squarely on the practical essentials and keep the jargon to an absolute minimum.

Why do I want to build my own computer?

Why indeed? You didn't build your own house, your own car or your own television – so why on earth would you want to build your own computer?

That's not entirely a rhetorical question, despite the nature of this book. We certainly don't want to turn you into a geek and life is surely too short to fuss with unnecessary projects for the sake of it. But the odd thing is, the more you learn about how computers tick and what goes into their construction, the less inclined you are to buy one.

It's not just that PCs are over-priced or over-complicated, although they are certainly both, but more that there's precious little to choose between a big brand name, a discount warehouse and someone selling anonymous hardware on a trestle table at the local computer market. Computers are 95% generic. The same few companies make most of the kit used in most of the world's PCs. This kit is accessible to all. Given all of which, there surely comes a point where it must make sense to at least think about doing it yourself. How hard can it be?

Perfection inspection

Well, presumably you are ready to take the plunge, and the happy news is that it's not hard at all. The surprising truth is that anyone can bolt together a computer, given the right parts, as we shall demonstrate. The trick, though, is getting the right parts, so to begin with we will run through all the main components.

Even if you decide not to build your own system, after reading this you will at least be better placed to buy a new system with

confidence. One glance at a superstore's displays will convince you that one computer does not fit all – and believe us, they don't carry all that stock with dozens of subtle permutations for the fun of it. But you don't have to compromise on the specification or be brow-beaten into paying over the odds for a bog-standard system; you can custom-build your own computer, from the motherboard to the mouse.

Our goal here is to help you build the 'perfect PC'. This, we suggest, fits the following criteria:

It must be suitable That is, it must be the right kind of computer for you. It's as simple as that, really: if you want to play games, you need powerful hardware in the multimedia department; and if you just want to plot your family tree and enjoy the benefits of e-mail, you really don't need wireless networking.

It must be flexible Your new computer should cover all the main bases from the outset. It must comfortably exceed the requirements of any software you care to throw at it and you should, for instance, be able to use a DVD encyclopaedia as easily as listen to an audio CD (or, indeed, make your own CD and DVD compilations). We'll help you work out what's important. But your habits will doubtless evolve over time and new software developments are forever expanding the horizon.

Who knows what you'll do with your computer a year from now? Which is why ...

It must be expandable The PC you build today, however basic or however fancy, must still meet your needs tomorrow. This requires some careful planning now and a strict adherence to industry standards. Come the day you wish to add to its features or boost its performance, an upgrade should be a pushover. True, you can never completely future-proof a PC but you can start with a solid base that will grow with you for years to come. Moreover ...

It must be affordable Any mug can walk into a computer shop with upwards of £1,000 and emerge with a 'ready for anything' computer. But how many of its features, all of which you've paid for, will you actually use? Is all that 'free' software really a bargain? Would you perhaps have settled for a little less in the way of performance in favour of a larger monitor? The trick is scaling down or cutting back on the optional extras and concentrating instead on the core. Again, you – not the manufacturer's marketing department and not the store sales team – determine what kind of computer you really need ... and how much you are prepared to pay for it.

If this all sounds like your kind of computer, read on.

PART

BUILD YOUR OWN COMPUTER

Planning the perfect PC

By doing all the donkey work yourself, you might justly assume that you can build a new computer for less than you'd pay in the shops. The truth may surprise you: you probably can't. But before you return this manual to the bookstore in a fit of pique, consider both the reasons why ... and the reasons why it doesn't matter.

PART ① Four good reasons to build your own computer

While it's true that you can buy precisely the same components from a retail outlet as an OEM (see p.12) can source direct from the manufacturer, you pay a considerable premium. It's not a level playing field, with the result that it can cost rather more to build your own system than to buy an off-the-peg identikit computer. And yet there are four good reasons why this really doesn't matter. These, indeed, are the reasons why we wrote this manual.

UNBEATABLE OFFER

Athlon XP 5000+++ Processor!
Massive 256MB DDR SD-RAM
Super-Big 60GB Hard Disk (5,400rpm)
Combo 52/ 48/12/6/2/1 x CD-R/RW/DVD+R/+RW

2 x USB Ports + Modem!   Integrated Audio!!!!
15-inch TFT Monitor!!   Six Speakers!!!!!
Integrated Graphics!!!   £££s free software!!!!!!

CALL NOW 0800 ~~345~~

Bargain of the century or a duff deal in disguise? If you've ever browsed the adverts and waded through specs, you'll know just how confusing buying a computer can be. So don't do it. Build one instead.

1. Satisfaction

Building your own computer is an immensely satisfying project. You're about to construct something from scratch that few people, even those who use them day in and day out, perhaps even you yourself, really understand. If that's not worth a pat on the back and a cup of kudos, we don't know what is.

2. Knowledge

To build a computer, you have to understand how everything fits together and be able sort out the important specifications from the marketing hype. When an advert proudly proclaims 'Blazing Pentium 4 3GHz+++ power!!!', and you can't believe the price, you can be sure that corners have been cut somewhere. But where, exactly? The answer is usually buried deep within the detailed specifications or hidden altogether: integrated graphics without an expansion slot for future upgrades, perhaps, or a cheap and nasty sound card, or insufficient memory. Read this manual in full and you'll know precisely where to look; build your own computer and you'll never be sold short again. The practical experience you'll gain in a DIY project of this nature is all you'll ever need to tackle computers with confidence for years to come.

3. Save money

Yes, despite what we said above, you can build a new PC on the cheap. The problem computer manufacturers and retailers alike face is one of having to be seen to offer the very latest kit at all times and at all cost – and that cost is borne by you, the consumer. But you don't necessarily need the latest kit, so why pay over the odds for PC performance that you'll never exploit? The key is compromising where you can and not where you shouldn't. By opting for a slightly slower processor and upping the ante elsewhere, you can make a PC that will outperform its shop-bought equivalent in every area – and save you money into the bargain.

4. It's the only PC you'll ever need

A bold claim indeed but one we feel confident in making. There are two really important points about building your own computer: you get to design it from the ground up to do precisely what you want it to do and, provided you start from a sound base, you can expand, upgrade, re-equip and otherwise enhance your computer more or less forever. Flexibility is the key.

The ultimate upgrade: replacing an outmoded – or broken – motherboard. But rather that, surely, than shelling out on a whole new system.

Pull the other one

But surely my computer will be out of date in a year anyway, you cry? Well, let's just examine that notion for a moment. Bits of it may no longer meet your changing needs, that is true, but the point is that you can upgrade your hardware to suit. It's never possible to predict changes in technology with absolute certainty but we can at least say that the SATA and PCI Express interfaces are here now and here to stay (more of which anon). All you have to do is choose a motherboard that supports the very latest technology – even if you don't actually *need* this technology right away – to guarantee a measure of future-proofing. An upgrade down the line is always going to be much, much cheaper than the cost of a new system so spending a few extra pounds now on a state-of-the-art motherboard has to be worthwhile.

Or let's imagine that a drive gives up the ghost somewhere down the line. No matter: a hardware failure is a temporary inconvenience, not a reason to replace your PC. Because you built the system in the first place, you'll know just how to fix it.

Even if one day you have to replace the motherboard in order to acquire new interfaces, you can probably reuse the case, power supply, some expansion cards and drives, plus the keyboard, mouse, monitor and everything else. The notion that computers must be replaced every two or three years to keep pace with advancing technology may fuel the industry and keep the tills ringing, but it's largely a marketing myth. Are you really inclined to treat something that costs between £500 and £1,500 as a mere 'commodity', a disposable mod con with a useful lifespan measured in months?

The downside?

Well … you will have to buy your operating system and application software separately instead of getting it bundled with a new system. This means extra expense. Then again, the software thrown in with new computers isn't really free; the cost is merely hidden within the system price and you could end up paying unwittingly for several programs that you don't really want and would never dream of purchasing separately.

Nor do you get an all-encompassing service contract, warranty or technical support when you build your own PC. But would you rather do without your computer for a week or more while it's away getting repaired – or fix it yourself in an hour? Besides, every component you buy will come with its own full warranty.

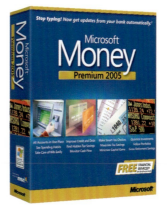

New systems generally come with Windows and a few applications – some of them even useful – pre-installed. When you build your own PC, remember to factor in the cost of new software.

PART ① PLANNING THE PERFECT PC

How to shop

Most PCs are constructed with components that are readily available on the open market. There's no great secret to it, really: all you need is a case, a power supply, a motherboard and a bunch of expansion cards and drives. True, some major-league manufacturers use proprietary parts that bind you to them for the lifetime of the computer – i.e. there's no other way to get spares and upgrades – but we're not concerned with such nonsense here.

An OEM would scoff at pretty packaging but there's a lot to be said for a retail product that gives you everything you need in the box. A motherboard, for instance, should include hard and floppy drive cables, a heatsink retention frame, installation screws, an I/O shield, chipset drivers, a manual and a warranty.

OEM vs retail

An OEM is a company that builds and sells computer systems with parts sourced from other companies. With access to the same parts, you can put together a system just as easily as any mass manufacturer. Indeed, should you wish to, you could put together the very same system. But better still, you can build the perfect PC for you: not necessarily the fastest computer on the block or the cheapest, but one that's custom-built to serve your needs both now and in the future.

There's really only one difference between components used by industry and those sold to consumers, and that's in the packaging. Consumer products sport fancy boxes and fancier price tags and fill the shelves of superstores,. You get everything you need in the box, including screws, cables, driver software and possibly an application or two. But an OEM has no need for frills and fripperies; rather, it buys bare components in bulk. A 'boxed' or 'retail' or 'consumer' (the terms mean the same thing in this context) Pentium or Athlon processor comes with a compatible heatsink and an instruction manual. The OEM buys exactly the same processor in trays of 1,000 with no extras whatsoever. Guess who pays less?

You, the intrepid system-builder, are not supposed to be able to get your hands on OEM stock, but it does filter its way through to specialist shops, direct vendors and computer fairs. So long as you're prepared to obtain your own cables, fittings, drivers and sundry other bits and bobs, an OEM component is usually a very good buy indeed.

When a power supply unit's air vents looks like this, you can be sure it has been round the block a few times. Nothing a blast of compressed air won't clear, of course, but you have to wonder how much life it has left.

New vs old

You can buy computer components from many different sources. The first obvious distinction is between new and old, about which we need say little. A used expansion card, drive, power supply or even motherboard may well perform absolutely perfectly for years to come, or it may already be five minutes removed from hardware heaven. Truth is, it's usually impossible to tell just by looking. Buyer beware – big time.

By their very nature, used components are not cutting-edge. This is absolutely fine: you might, for instance, want to build a basic workstation for web surfing, e-mail, word processing and perhaps a little image editing and printing. Such a system requires only a relatively modest specification – even a Pentium II-based machine will be fine – and it would be wasteful and pointless to build-in surround sound and 3D graphics.

However, there are two important caveats. First, your computer will not be particularly amenable to future upgrades. Should it need a serious performance boost to keep pace with your changing habits, you won't be able to swap out the processor for a Pentium 4 or add an extra slice of fast DDR-RAM or slot in a 8x-speed AGP card for gaming. You might not even be able to add a large hard disk drive as older BIOS programs don't always recognise or work with today's monoliths. Windows XP won't run on less than a 233MHz processor (and that's very optimistic indeed) so you'll likely be stuck with an older, less-adept operating system.

Now, all of this is fine so long as you know what you're getting into. Bottom line: today's bargain-basement project is unlikely to serve you well if you need a supercomputer tomorrow.

Also, and this might rather pain you, you can almost certainly pick up a complete, well-worn but perfectly serviceable second-hand computer system for much less than the cost of building one from scratch. Check the small ads, use an online auction site such as eBay, try a reconditioned computer specialist such as Morgan or just ask around. Chances are you can pick one up for a song, perhaps sold without a monitor or extras like the keyboard and mouse. End result? A basic but functional and upgradeable-to-a-degree computer that's worth several times the price of its parts.

And so ...

In short, when building rather than buying a computer, we believe it makes sense to adopt the very latest technology in several key interrelated areas, notably the motherboard, processor and memory. With up-to-date components at the heart of your system, a degree of future-proofing is guaranteed. Everything else, from the mouse to the monitor, from the scanner to the sound card, can be a compromise.

Older but still-functional computers are regularly replaced by individuals and industry alike. Shop around at an online auction site like eBay and you'll certainly find some bargains. Look out for pitfalls, though: an office-based machine may lack a sound card and speakers, and you should check whether the hard disk has been wiped clean of software.

PART **1** Where to shop

Several types of retailer are contenders for your component cash.

Computer superstores

Superstores cater more for people in the market for a ready-made computer or perhaps replacement drive or peripheral than the screwdriver-wielding DIY system-builder. Prices can be exceptionally good on certain lines – take advantage of special offers – but extras like printer cables can attract premium rates.

High street independents

A mixed bunch, in our experience. Many smaller shops are staffed with clued-up enthusiasts happy to offer advice and help you with a purchase. Others are not.

Mail order/web vendors

Having lower overheads than 'real' shops, mail order and internet companies (often one and the same) should be able to offer better prices. They generally do just that, but remember to factor in delivery charges. Some also offer OEM goods, so check whether you're about to order a boxed, consumer-friendly retail product with a manual – or a drive-in-a-bag.

Dabs.com is one of the largest online high-tech retailers in the UK. Its extensive Dabsvalue range includes unbranded OEM-style products at rock-bottom prices.

Superstores like PC World offer a good selection of DIY components alongside complete computer systems. Check the Bargain Zones for the best deals.

Snapping up bargains at a computer fair stall. See Appendix 4 for details of websites that list local markets.

Computer fair

Computer fairs are held regularly up and down the country. Here you will find the best prices of all, as long as you're prepared to haggle a little. However, the prospect of handing over a large wad of cash to a trader you fear you may never see again is rather daunting. Our advice is to leave your wallet at home the first time you visit your local fair. Get the feel of the place, note the traders' names and jot down some representative prices. You can compare these with shop prices later. By all means have a chat with a few traders and suss out who's prepared to offer free advice and a no-quibble return guarantee.

Official monthly fairs are policed by the organisers, and regular traders do tend to be trustworthy. You will certainly find OEM stock at a fair, and also salvaged components plucked from old PCs. If you need a stick of SD-RAM for an old motherboard, a fair is the good bet – as indeed it is for that old motherboard in the first place.

Golden rules include:

● Only deal with traders who openly display a landline telephone number (not just a mobile number) and address.

● Establish your right of return with the trader before paying, and check how you would go about making a return. Will you have to wait a month or more before you see the trader again?

● Keep all packaging and receipts.

B-grade stock

Damaged goods, items returned by customers without the original packaging, end-of-line components that have to make shelf room for newer stock, used systems sold off by companies upgrading their IT departments ... all manner of functional but not-quite-perfect items qualify as 'B-grade'. The one constant factor is that this stuff is sold at a healthy discount.

You should get a guarantee of sorts with a B-grade item – perhaps 30 or 90 days – and (a matter of importance) any deficiencies should be clearly stated at the point of purchase. You have every right to get your money back if your purchase is dodgy in any way you weren't adequately forewarned about.

Take care, though. A monitor with a cracked screen isn't a terribly bright buy, nor is a fire-damaged power supply unit. But a sound card sold without a box, cables, drivers or manual might be a sensible cost-cutting investment.

And so ...

Above all, shop around. Component prices vary wildly from place to place, often without rhyme or reason. Use a credit card wherever possible to take advantage of the added protection. Bone up on your consumer rights, too, just in case of problems. See Appendix 4 for contacts.

PART 1 Hard and soft options

In the next section, we'll look at the main components that go together to make a computer. But first you must decide what type of computer you wish to build.

Matching hardware to software

If there was a magic formula – 'to do X and Y buy Z' – we would print it here. Sadly there isn't – but then you can't just walk into a shop and buy the 'perfect PC' straight off the shelf. Nor can we provide you with a definitive buying guide or make specific product recommendations. For one thing, any such advice would be instantly out of date; for another, one of the great secrets of computer design is that it matters far, far less which brand name you buy than whether a given component adheres to industry standards (no proprietary parts here, thank you very much) and has the right specification for its intended purpose. As a system-builder, you have the opportunity – nay, the luxury – of being able to make informed choices about every single part of your computer.

We will talk you through the hardware in Part 2. However, the old adage of horses for courses holds true in the software stakes too: the computer you build must be well-suited to its end use. You don't need a room-sized mainframe to surf the web any more than you need seven satellite speakers and a sub-woofer to keep track of your household finances, but you do need a good deal of processing power and a swanky video card if you want to play computer games (plus a joystick, a powerful sound card and probably a set of headphones to keep the neighbours sweet).

Recommended system requirements

Application type	Typical example	Processor speed (MHz)	Memory (MB)	Hard disk space (MB)	Other requirements
Operating system	Windows XP Home Edition	300	128	1,500	
Office applications	Microsoft Office 2003 Pro	233	256	790	
Image editor	Jasc Paint Shop Pro	500	128	75	
DVD movie player	CyberLink PowerDVD	400	64	40	DVD drive
Digital video editor	Pinnacle Studio 9	800	512	500	FireWire/USB port to connect a camcorder; lots of hard disk space for storing raw video
Digital media	Roxio Creator 7	500	256	1,000	Recordable CD or DVD drive
Game	Medal of Honor: Pacific Assault	1,500	512	3,000	Video card with 128MB memory
Desktop publishing	CorelDRAW Graphics Suite 12	200	128	250	
Reference	Encyclopaedia Britannica 2004	350	256	400	
Antivirus	Norton Antivirus 2005	300	128	125	
Utility suite	Norton SystemWorks 2005	300	128	150	

In all cases, we assume the presence of a monitor, mouse, keyboard, sound card, speakers, a CD drive from which to install the software and an internet connection.

Changing pace

Computer hardware and software have long played a game of catch-up with one another but not always in the same direction. A few years ago, for instance, it was common for software applications to stretch hardware capability to breaking point. This was especially true in the realm of gaming. Then, for a while, hardware performance leapt ahead and the average desktop PC was much more powerful than we actually needed it to be. Real multitasking, by which we mean being able to run several intensive applications simultaneously, became the norm. Even the humblest mass-production shop-bought system could handle having a web browser, e-mail program, word processor, encyclopaedia and desktop publishing program all open at the same time with surplus capacity aplenty.

By and large, the power balance has shifted little. To make the point, we've listed a few typical applications along with their recommended hardware specifications in the following table. Now, nothing here will remotely stretch any PC that you're liable to buy or build today. Indeed, only one of our sample applications specifies so much as a 1.5GHz processor – they're currently running upwards of twice as fast – and you're unlikely to be pushed for hard disk space with today's 200GB drives. The game's requirement for a hefty video card is the only potential sticking point.

Memory matters

But it's not *quite* as straightforward as all that. Perhaps the most noticeable and certainly the most significant thing about these figures is the importance of memory. The overall quantity of RAM in a system – and to a lesser extent the *type* of RAM chosen – has a huge bearing on that system's overall performance, especially when it comes to multitasking. It's one thing for a computer to run 17 programs at the same time but quite another for it to do so smoothly without locking-up or hanging the system. Given that multitasking is a PC's forte, or should be, and that you shouldn't have to shut down programs A and B before firing up programs C, D and E, it's sensible to install considerably more RAM than you think you need in order to keep things ticking along nicely. Compromise in almost every other area before skimping on memory.

Processors matter too

Moreover, these system requirements mask the fact that in certain key areas software is now once again pushing at the boundaries of hardware. Computer gaming is one obvious area where it's beneficial if not downright essential to have a fast processor, stacks of memory and the very latest souped-up video card at your disposal. Anything less and you won't see your games play to their full potential. Frame rates drop and detail is lost.

But even if you're not interested in games, consider digital video. This is another key area where the possibilities can be hampered by hardware limitations. For instance, a PC makes a fabulous video editing suite if you have a camcorder. You can transfer raw footage to the hard disk and tweak and transform it into a polished home movie. You can then publish your efforts on a website, share them via e-mail or make your own DVDs. Even basic video editing software is spectacularly powerful (including Windows Movie Maker, which comes free with Windows XP). For the amateur film-maker, these are happy days. However, the harsh reality is that you need pretty sturdy hardware to work with digital video at a comfortable pace. Just about any PC can edit and produce a movie, but not all can do it while you wait. A slow system will take hours to render a movie (i.e. apply your edits, captions, effects and so forth to raw footage and produce a finished file), and some will need all night and perhaps well into the following morning. While it's engaged in the business of rendering, there's not much else you can do with your computer short of chivvying it along with words of encouragement or, more likely, frustration.

If movie-making appeals, don't skimp on processing power.

Bottom line: if video is your thing, invest in a speedy processor to cut the waiting time to a minimum.

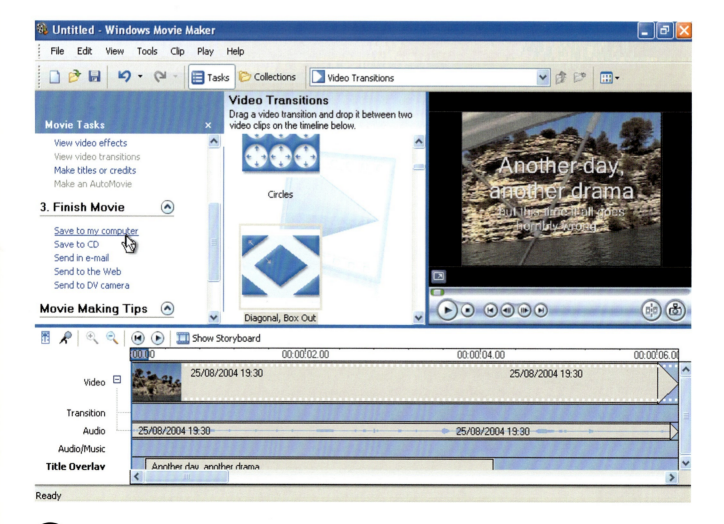

Beige be gone

Much to the amusement of Mac fans, for whom form is almost as important as function, most PC manufacturers now have a stab at making their products attractive. Usually, they fail dismally, but you, the system builder, can have a much better go at this yourself.

We'll build two very different PCs in the course of this book, one of which would look perfectly at home in a living room setting. This is an example of a 'small form factor' PC, which is what you'll likely want if you intend to build a home entertainment centre.

A what, you wonder? Well, odd though it may sound, a suitably configured PC connected to a TV can effectively replace your video recorder, DVD player, stereo system and games console. It can also showcase digital images, import and export media to and from other computers in a home network, and generally function as the very hub of your home entertainment. Forget the keyboard and mouse; all you need is a remote control. Skip to Appendix 2 now for more details. Meanwhile, just bear in mind as you go along that the PC has finally made the leap from the study to the sitting room. You are in the enviable position of being able to design and build an ideal system from scratch.

Our other project PC caters more for future expansion and flexibility but it's no mean looker for all that. It would also be ideally suited to the next step in system-building, which is customising or 'modding' (modifying) a PC for maximum effect. We're talking cut-away Perspex panels that showcase internal neon tube lights, swish water-cooling systems, solid gold heatsinks and that kind of thing. This, though, is subject matter for a different book.

But we're getting ahead of ourselves. Let's turn now to the nuts and bolts that you will use to build your computer.

Even now, not many PCs can compete with a Mac for styling. Then again, you can't build your own Mac.

2

PART **2**

BUILD YOUR OWN COMPUTER

Choosing your hardware

Inevitably, this section gets rather technical but, as always, we'll focus on what you really need to know and resist wallowing in the mire of jargon and the inner workings of microelectronics. You don't need to know that Intel's 4004 processor ran at a clock speed of 108KHz in 1971 to appreciate that today's Pentium 4 3.06GHz processor – some 28,000 times faster than the 4004 – is particularly well-suited to ultra-demanding software applications but is definite overkill for the odd spreadsheet.

PART 2 Motherboard

The single most important piece of hardware that you will buy is the motherboard – the very heart of your system. The processor plugs into it, drives connect to it with cables, expansion cards live in special slots and everything else, from the mouse to the printer, is ultimately connected to and controlled by the motherboard. If you buy a PC from a shop, chances are you'll never think about or even see the motherboard; but when you build a system from scratch, it must be your primary consideration. Everything else follows from here.

A sample motherboard

Here's a close look at the motherboard we'll be using in the first of our projects. It's pretty much state of the art.

Memory slots	For installing memory modules
Processor socket	For installing the processor
Chipset (Northbridge)	The motherboard's control centre
Parallel	For connecting a printer
PS/2 (2)	For connecting a mouse and keyboard
S/PDIF in/out	For importing and exporting digital audio signals
RJ45 (2)	For connecting a wired local area network (LAN)
USB (4)	For connecting peripheral devices
Audio (6)	For connecting speakers (7.1 surround sound), a line-in device and a microphone
Wi-Fi	For connecting a wireless networking receiver
PCI Express 16x	For installing a video card

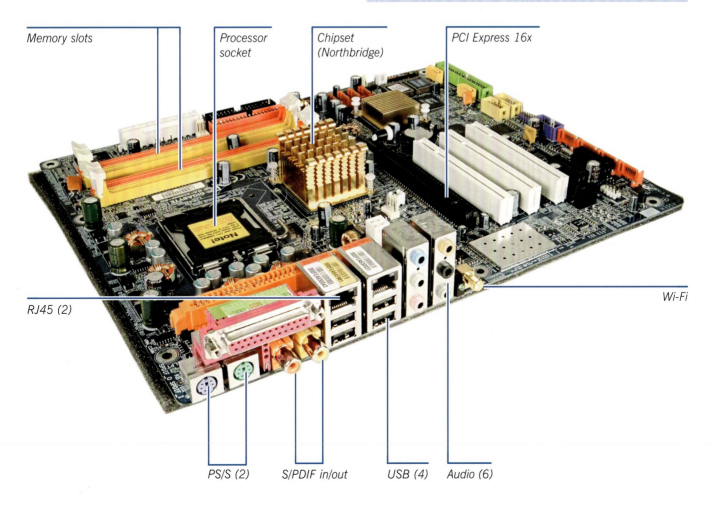

Memory slots

Processor socket

Chipset (Northbridge)

PCI Express 16x

RJ45 (2)

Wi-Fi

PS/S (2)

S/PDIF in/out

USB (4)

Audio (6)

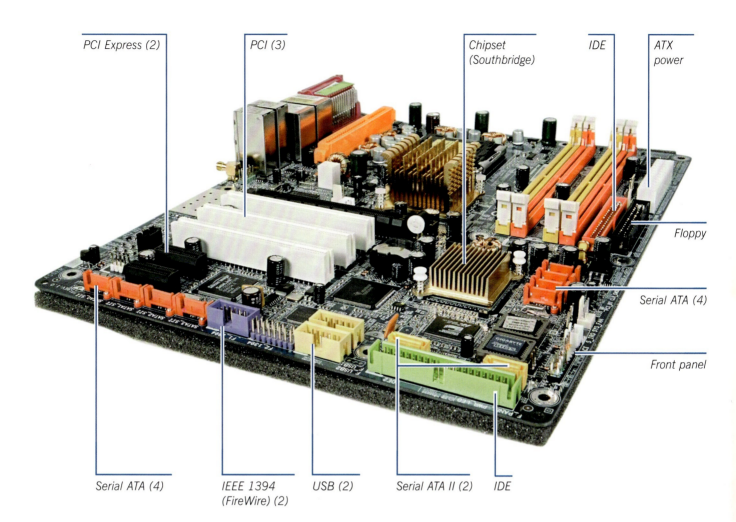

PCI Express (2)   PCI (3)   Chipset (Southbridge)   IDE   ATX power

Floppy

Serial ATA (4)

Front panel

Serial ATA (4)   IEEE 1394 (FireWire) (2)   USB (2)   Serial ATA II (2)   IDE

QUICK Q&A

I'm considering a motherboard that claims to be 'legacy-free'. It sounds like a bonus but what does it mean?

It means it has no serial, parallel, mouse or keyboard ports and nowhere to connect a floppy disk drive! This might be a good thing but only if you already have or intend to get a USB mouse, keyboard, printer, etc. and don't mind going without a floppy drive. It's certainly the way of the future. For this project, we couldn't quite bring ourselves to ditch these legacy interfaces just yet.

PCI (3)	For installing standard expansion cards
PCI Express (2)	For installing the latest, fastest expansion cards
Serial ATA (8)	For connecting new-style hard drives
IEEE 1394 (FireWire) (2)	For connecting via a FireWire cable to a drive or device
USB (2)	For connecting via a USB cable to a drive or device
Serial ATA II (2)	For connecting high-speed new-style hard drives
IDE (2)	For connecting old-style hard drives
Front panel	For connecting lights and buttons on the front of the case
Chipset (Southbridge)	The motherboard's control centre
Floppy	For connecting a floppy drive
ATX power	For connecting the power supply unit

And another one

This motherboard is an older model but representative of the kind of thing you could easily pick up for a song at a computer fair. We've highlighted the key differences.

AGP	This special slot is used to install the video card. Gradually, the AGP standard is being superseded by the superior PCI Express standard.	Memory slots	The difference here is not obvious to the eye but the newer motherboard can run memory in dual-channel configuration whereas this model can not. For the benefits, see p.46.
PCI	This motherboard has six PCI slots for adding expansion cards, whereas the newer model on the previous pages has but three. However, the newer model also has two PCI Express slots which can host faster, more powerful expansion cards. It also has both wired (LAN) and wireless (Wi-Fi) connections built-in, plus a powerful on-board multi-channel audio chip with a stack of inputs and outputs. This means that you simply don't need as many expansion cards.	IDE	There are two IDE sockets on this motherboard, each of which can host two hard drives or optical CD/DVD drives. The computer can thus have a maximum of four internal drives. On the new model, we still find the IDE sockets, but these are rapidly disappearing in favour of the Serial ATA standard (for which there are no fewer than ten sockets). It's useful to have an IDE socket or two around, if only for reusing existing hard or optical drives, but SATA is the way forward.
Processor socket	Here we see a Socket 478 socket for a Pentium 4 processor. On the newer motherboard, this has been replaced by the LGA775 Pentium 4 socket. As we shall see, the design of processor sockets (and, before that, slots) is ever-changing, which generates a whole bunch of compatibility issues.		

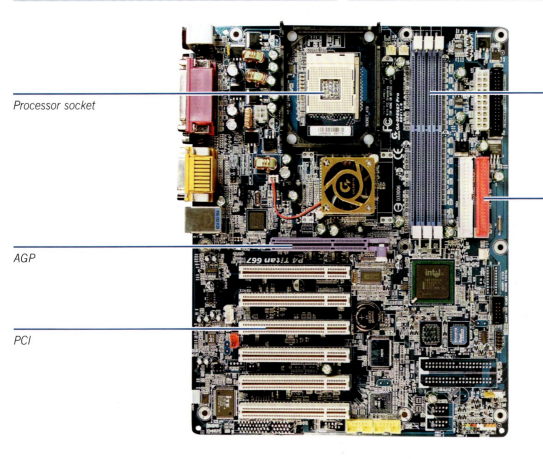

Processor socket

Memory slots

IDE

AGP

PCI

Form factor

This is a fancy way of describing a motherboard's size and shape, important because it involves industry-wide standards and ties in with the computer case and power supply. Form factors have evolved through the years, culminating since 1995 in a popular and flexible standard known as ATX. Not just one ATX standard, of course: there are MiniATX, MicroATX and FlexATX motherboards out there, all progressively slimmed-down versions of full-size ATX. The upside of a smaller motherboard is that you can use a smaller case and reduce the overall dimensions of your computer; the downside is a corresponding reduction in expandability. A full-sized ATX motherboard can have up to seven expansion slots while a MicroATX motherboard is limited to four.

Should you have a tape measure handy and wish to do some checking, here are the maximum ATX motherboard board sizes as specified by Intel:

ATX	305mm	x	244mm
MiniATX	284mm	x	208mm
MicroATX	244mm	x	244mm
FlexATX	229mm	x	191mm

One technical benefit of ATX over the earlier BabyAT form factor from which it directly evolved is that full-length expansion cards can now be fitted in all slots; previously, the location of the processor and memory on the motherboard meant that some slots could only take stumpy (not a technical term) cards. Another is the use of a double-height input/output panel that lets motherboard manufacturers build-in more integrated features. All in all, it's a definite improvement.

But from your point of view, the main attraction has to be the guarantee that any ATX motherboard, including the smaller versions, will fit inside any ATX computer case. That's the beauty of standards.

The most recent mainstream addition to the form factor parade is BTX (Balanced Technology Extended). This has a leaner, flatter form factor compared to ATX, and is specifically designed to facilitate adequate cooling in smaller computers, especially those designed for home entertainment. A BTX motherboard comes in three variations:

BTX	267mm	x	325mm
MicroBTX	267mm	x	263mm
PicoBTX	267mm	x	203mm

Beyond BTX, you can also buy Mini-ITX motherboards from a manufacturer called VIA (**www.viaembedded.com**). These are square in shape, 170mm x 170mm, and designed primarily for squeezing into strictly non-standard computer projects. As Wikipedia (**http://en.wikipedia.org/wiki/Mini-itx**) puts it:

Today, Mini-ITX is used by hobbyists to build not only embedded computers, but also to build computers in nearly any object that will house it. Hollowed out vintage computers, humidors, toys, electronics, a guitar, and even a 1960s-era toaster have become homes to relatively quiet, or even silent Mini-ITX systems, capable of many of the tasks of a modern desktop PC.

For examples and inspiration, see **www.mini-itx.com**.

Next in line comes the even smaller 120mm x 120mm Nano-ITX form factor. Like Mini-ITX, this is developed exclusively by VIA with the aim of making even smaller, but still fully functional, PCs possible.

A really very tiny indeed 12cm-square Nano-ITX motherboard from VIA.

The chipset

The real meat of a motherboard resides in its chipset: a collection of microchips that together control all the major functions. Without a chipset, a motherboard would be lifeless; with a duff chipset, it may be inadequate for your needs. Indeed, as one motherboard manufacturer explained it to us, the chipset *is* the motherboard: don't ask what this or that motherboard can do – ask instead what chipset it uses and there you'll find your answer.

So what does a chipset do, precisely? Well, at one level it controls the flow of data between motherboard components through a series of interfaces. Each interface, or channel, is called a bus. The most important buses are:

FSB (Front Side Bus) The interface between the Northbridge component of the chipset and the processor.

Memory bus The interface between the chipset and RAM.

AGP (Accelerated Graphics Port) The interface between the chipset and the AGP port. This is gradually disappearing from motherboards as more and more video cards are designed for the PCI Express slot.

PCI (Peripheral Component Interconnect) bus The interface between the chipset and PCI expansion slots. Pretty much any expansion card can be installed here, including sound cards, network cards and TV tuners. The exception is a video card, as these are, or were, designed for the higher bandwidth AGP interface. Like AGP, PCI is gradually giving way to PCI Express.

PCI Express bus The interface between the chipset and PCI Express expansion slots. There may be two separate buses determined by the bandwidth of the slots. For instance, the motherboard may have a 16-speed PCI Express slot for the video card and one or more slower slots for standard expansion cards.

IDE (Integrated Drive Electronics) bus The interface between the chipset and hard/optical drives.

SATA (Serial Advanced Technology Attachment) bus An alternative interface between the chipset and hard/optical drives which will eventually completely replace the IDE bus.

And then there are buses controlling the floppy disk drive, parallel and serial ports, USB and FireWire, integrated audio, and more.

Here we have a Pentium 4 processor (left), an 82925XE Northbridge or Memory Controller Hub chip (top right) and an ICR6H Southbridge or Input/Output Controller Hub chip. Which is quite some mouthful. But put them together and you'll have a motherboard with an Intel 925XE chipset.

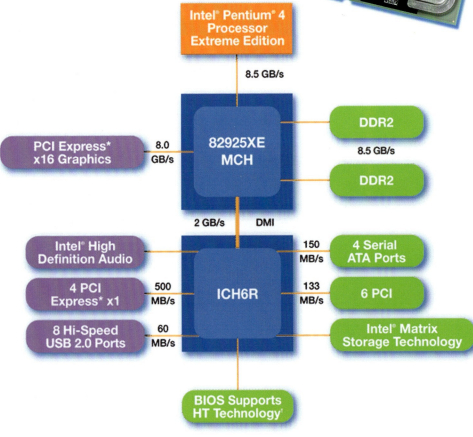

The same chipset viewed schematically. Note how the Northbridge (MCH) and Southbridge (ICH) chips have different responsibilities.

Bus bandwidths

Not all buses are equal. Far from it, in fact: they operate at different speeds and have different 'widths'. For example, the basic single-speed (1x) AGP specification has a clock speed of 66.6MHz (usually expressed as 66MHz). This means that over 66 million units of data can pass between the video card and the chipset through the bus per second. However, the AGP bus transfers 32 bits of data (that's 32 individual 1s and 0s) with every clock cycle, so the true measure of the bus is not its speed alone but rather the overall rate at which data is transferred. This is known as the bandwidth of a bus. In this case, 32 bits pass through the bus 66 million times per second. This equates to a bandwidth of 266MB/sec.

Just to be clear, using round figures, here's the sum:

66,600,000 clock cycles x 32 bits = 2,131,200,000 bits/sec

There are 8 bits in a byte (B), so this equals 266,400,000 B/sec

There are 1,000 bytes in a kilobyte (KB), so this equals 266,400 KB/sec

There are 1,000 kilobytes in a megabyte (MB), so this equals 266 MB/sec

Looked at another way, the AGP bus transfers sufficient data to fill a recordable CD every three seconds.

It's also possible to run the AGP bus up to eight times faster, which boosts the bandwidth to over 2 gigabytes per sec. This is the kind of speed you need for playing games. By contrast, the PCI bus runs at only 133MB/sec. This is fine for many purposes but not for three-dimensional video.

Now consider the bandwidth of an 800MHz front side bus on a motherboard designed for a Pentium 4 processor. The bus itself is 64 bits wide – that is, 64 bits are transferred every second – and the clock 'ticks' 800 million times per second. This equates to a bandwidth of 6,400MB/sec, or very nearly fast enough to fill a DVD with data in a second.

Some buses can transfer data two, four or eight times per clock cycle, which effectively doubles, quadruples etc. the overall bandwidth. The new PCI Express standard allows for multiple 'lanes' which pump data in a number of simultaneous streams. The upshot is that PCI Express is vastly superior to that of PCI or even AGP 8x-speed.

If all this makes your head spin, put away your calculator and consult the following table instead. We'll save the thrill of memory bus bandwidths for later (see p.47).

Some bus bandwidths

	Bus name	Bandwidth (MB/sec)
FSB (Pentium 4)	400MHz	3,200
	533MHz	4,266
	800MHz	6,400
	1,066MHz	8,500
Expansion slots	PCI	133
	AGP	266
	AGP 2x	533
	AGP 4x	1,066
	AGP 8x	2,133
	PCI Express 1x	500
	PCI Express 2x	1,000
	PCI Express 4x	2,000
	PCI Express 8x	4,000
	PCI Express 16x	8,000
Drive interfaces	IDE/ATA-33	33
	IDE/ATA-66	66
	IDE/ATA-100	100
	IDE/ATA-133	133
	SATA I	150
	SATA II	300

Chipset architecture

We needn't linger on the physical design of chipsets except to comment briefly on the terminology you are likely to encounter:

● **Northbridge** The primary chip in a chipset, it typically controls the processor, memory and video buses.

● **Southbridge** A second chip that typically incorporates the PCI, IDE/SATA and USB buses.

● **Super I/O** A third, subsidiary chip that usually supports the floppy disk drive, serial ports and a parallel port, and sometimes also the mouse and keyboard ports.

However, these associations between bus and chip are far from immutable. Moreover, Intel recently switched to a 'hub architecture' where the Northbridge chip is called the Memory Controller Hub and the Southbridge is the I/O Controller Hub. AMD, that other processor-producing giant, refers to Northbridge and Southbridge chips as the System Controller and Peripheral Bus Controller respectively. More importantly, the latest Athlon 64 processor family incorporates the memory controller within the processor, thereby releasing the Northbridge chip from much of its responsibility.

From the buyer's perspective, it matters more what a chipset offers overall than how it does it.

Processor and memory support

The two most important questions with any motherboard, and hence computer, are which processor family and what kind of memory does it work with?

For instance, if you decide that you want to build a Pentium 4-based system, you'll need a motherboard with either a Socket 478 or a Socket 775 to house it; and if you want an Athlon-based system, you'll be looking for a Socket 939, 940 or 974. So far, so confusing. It gets all the more so when you factor in the many possible permutations of memory support, including bus speed, number of slots on the motherboard and whether it offers single-channel or dual-channel performance. We'll cover all of this in due course.

Need a further complication? Intel makes its own chipsets, which means it's easy to compare like for like, but AMD largely relies on third-party manufacturers to come up with compatible chipsets for its processors. There's nothing wrong with AMD's stance on this – and indeed it opens the market to chipset manufacturers which would otherwise be squeezed out by Intel's dominance – but it does make motherboard comparisons slightly trickier.

A Socket 939 Athlon 64 processor. We'll use this later in our small form factor PC project.

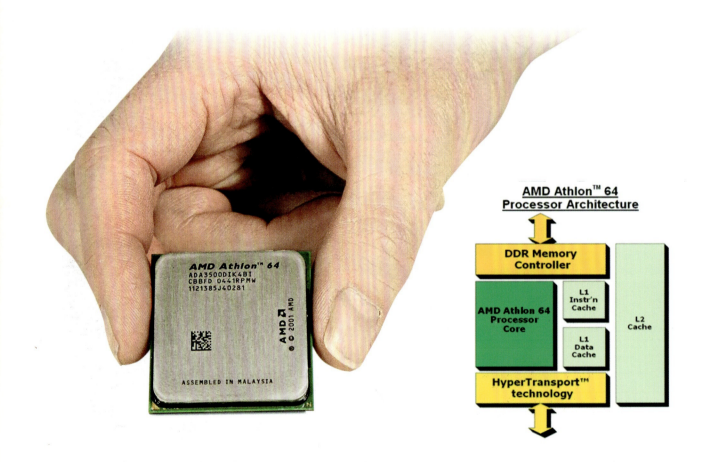

AMD Athlon™ 64
Processor Architecture

DDR Memory Controller

AMD Athlon 64 Processor Core

L1 Instr'n Cache

L1 Data Cache

L2 Cache

HyperTransport™ technology

Integrated multimedia

Another important feature of motherboards that again depends upon the chipset is the presence or otherwise of 'onboard' or 'integrated' sound and video. An integrated sound chip means that the motherboard can handle audio playback and recording without the need for a separate sound card. That is, you simply connect speakers and a microphone to outputs and inputs provided by the motherboard. Integrated video means you don't need a separate video card.

The attraction of this approach is primarily one of reduced cost: a motherboard with integrated sound and/or video saves the system-builder having to shell out for one or two pricey expansion cards. A motherboard with integrated multimedia features is thus a smart buy, right?

Well, not necessarily. Remember, we're building the 'perfect PC' here, one requirement of which is that it must be able to adapt to your changing needs. The drawback with integrated multimedia is that it potentially limits your upgrade options. Audio is rather less of an issue than video. Sound cards are always designed for the PCI expansion slot so it's possible to upgrade to a more powerful card later, assuming there is a free slot on the motherboard. The slight complication is that you must

disable the integrated sound chip before your sound card will work (see p.138).

It is also possible to disable integrated video in favour of an expansion card – but where will you install it? Some motherboards with integrated video have a vacant AGP or, more recently, PCI Express, slot for just this purpose, in which case there's no problem: simply disable the chip and install your video expansion card. However, others have no such slot, in which case you are, quite frankly, stuffed. Without a free slot, your only real option would be to install a slower PCI video card, but this would almost certainly be a downgrade. Unless you are very, very confident that you will never wish to upgrade your PC's video capabilities – in particular, that you'll never play computer games or change from an analogue to a digital monitor or wish to run two monitors simultaneously – only consider a motherboard with integrated video if it also has a vacant AGP or PCI Express slot. A small saving now may have serious consequences later.

Of course, there is another advantage to integration, namely reduced size. With the current trend towards smaller, sleeker, lighter, prettier PCs, it makes sense to incorporate as many functions as possible into the motherboard.

When both video and audio output are embedded on the motherboard, as in this small form factor example, the need for expansion slots is reduced. In fact, you may get away with none at all.

Sizing up the specifications

Intel chipsets

What we need here are some concrete examples. We've picked six Intel chipsets and listed their main features in order to highlight the differences between them.

	Intel 925XE Express	Intel 925X Express	Intel 915P	Intel 915GL	Intel 865P	Intel 845PE
Processor support	Intel Pentium 4	Intel Pentium 4	Intel Pentium 4	Intel Pentium 4	Intel Pentium 4	Intel Pentium 4
Processor socket	775	775	775	775	478	478
Front Side Bus (MHz)	1,066/800	800	800/533	800/533	533/400	533/400
Memory (RAM) support	Dual-channel DDR2	Dual-channel DDR2	Dual-channel DDR2 or DDR	Dual-channel DDR	Dual-channel DDR	Single-channel DDR
Memory bus (MHz)	533/400	533/400	533/400 (DDR2); 400/333 (DDR)	400/333	333/266	333/266
Memory slots	4	4	4	4	4	2
Maximum installable memory (GB)	4	4	4	4	4	2
PCI slots	6	6	6	6	6	6
PCI Express 16x-speed (for video card)	1	1	1	-	-	-
PCI Express	4	4	4	4	-	-
AGP slot	-	-	-	-	1	1
IDE sockets	2	2	2	2	-	2
SATA sockets	4	4	4	4	2	-
Integrated audio	Yes	Yes	Yes	Yes	Yes	Yes
Integrated graphics	-	-	-	Yes	-	-
Integrated LAN	Yes	Yes	Yes	Yes	Yes	Yes

A word of explanation

If you know what you're looking at, and for, it's possible to glean a good deal of useful information from bare specifications like these. We'll look at the first of these examples, the 925XE chipset, in detail again later and we'll be considering processors, memory and more over the coming pages. But for now, a little explanation might be helpful. What *are* we looking at in this table, exactly?

Processor support Which make and type of processor the motherboard supports. When building a desktop system, this almost always means either an Intel Pentium 4 or Celeron or an AMD Athlon or Sempron.

Processor socket This specifies the design of the motherboard socket. In the table, we can see that there are two possibilities: Socket 775 and Socket 478. Some older Pentium 4 processors used yet another design called Socket 423. The critical thing is to know which socket your motherboard has, for this determines which version of processor you should – indeed, must – purchase.

Front Side Bus (MHz) Effectively, this is the speed at which the processor communicates with the chipset and memory. The higher the number, the more efficient the processor. Cast an eye along this line and you'll see that the FSB figure varies from 400MHz to 1,066MHz. By now, it should be obvious that the processors on the left of the table are more powerful – which means newer – than those on the right. In fact, an FSB boost is the only significant difference between the 925XE and the 925X.

Memory (RAM) support See p.43–48 for the lowdown on memory. Meanwhile, simply note that there are two main flavours of RAM around, DDR and DDR2, and two ways of using it: single-channel or dual-channel mode. Dual-channel DDR2 is the current front-runner. In our table, the newer 925 chipsets are designed to accommodate the latest memory modules. The 865P chipset was developed before the time of DDR2, although it does offer dual-channel support for DDR modules. The older 845PE chipset can only handle DDR modules in single-channel configuration.

Memory bus (MHz) This is a similar story to the FSB. In practice, and budget permitting, you're going to want to source memory that exploits the full bandwidth of the motherboard's memory bus. Where a motherboard offers support for two buses – 533MHz and 400MHz, for example – you'll build a better system if you install memory modules that run at 533MHz.

Memory slots This determines how many memory modules you'll be able to install. It would be rare and daft for a motherboard manufacturer not to provide the full complement of slots.

Maximum installable memory (GB) This determines how much memory you can install. For instance, with four slots and support for 4GB, you could conceivably install four 1GB memory modules. Do you need this much memory? No, not really.

PCI slots The maximum number of PCI slots. Motherboard manufacturers are free to implement fewer and do so. This is one occasion to ignore the chipset specification and look instead at the motherboard specification.

PCI Express 16x-speed (for video card) If you want the latest in video power, which you will if you're building a games-laying PC, it's sensible to look for this slot. AGP is still very much with us but a year down the line it's likely that all new video cards will be designed for PCI Express. What you won't readily find is a motherboard with both PCI Express 16x-speed and AGP slots, although they do exist. The three most recent of our chipsets all now feature PCI Express for video.

PCI Express Going forward, non-video expansion cards, such as sound cards and network cards, are more likely to be developed for the PCI Express interface than for plain old PCI even when they don't actually need the extra bandwidth. A motherboard with both flavours is the best bet to ensure both that you can reuse any old cards that you already have or pick up cheaply and that you can install the latest cards a year down the line.

AGP slot See PCI Express 16x-speed above.

IDE sockets IDE sockets are still present on most modern motherboards, which is as it should be. After all, there are still millions of serviceable IDE hard disks around, and you way well want to install one or more for easy, cheap additional storage space. The latest DVD writers are still routinely made for the IDE interface, too, and we reckon it will be some time before IDE disappears completely. In extremis, however, you can use an adapter to fit an IDE drive to a SATA interface, so don't necessarily rule out an otherwise perfect motherboard if its sole shortcoming is the lack of an IDE socket or two.

SATA sockets The replacement for IDE. You should certainly ensure that your new motherboard has SATA sockets. See p.56 for details.

Integrated audio Virtually all motherboards feature integrated audio, which means you don't need to install a sound card. Of course, you *can* install a sound card and simply ignore the integrated audio if you like, as we'll discuss on p.61–62.

Integrated graphics The point of an integrated graphics chip is that you don't need to install a video card. However, while this is fine for two-dimensional work such as word processing and web browsing, it's fair to say that integrated chips are not usually up to gaming. If you see a G in an Intel chipset's name, as in our 915GL example, you can be assured that it includes integrated graphics. Otherwise, you're back to the choice between installing an AGP or a PCI Express video card – a choice that is obviously governed by the chipset and the motherboard's support for one or the other interface.

Integrated LAN You really don't want to waste a PCI slot or still less a PCI Express slot on a network card. Luckily, most chipsets provide built-in support which, in practice, means you'll find a network port or two ready for instant action in the motherboard's input/output panel (see p.22 for an example).

TECHIE CORNER

Chipset drivers You can't upgrade the chipset on an old motherboard but you can and should upgrade the chipset drivers periodically. Sometimes, motherboards are rushed to market and the software that controls the chipset – and hence the entire computer – doesn't work as it should. Sometimes it's downright broken. A driver update is often sufficient to bring the chipset up to speed and hence make the difference between a useful motherboard and a waste of money. Driver updates can also improve chipset performance in a key area such as integrated video. Pay occasional visits to the motherboard or chipset manufacturer's website and look for downloadable driver updates. We should also point out that the risk of running into driver and performance problems is significantly higher if you buy the very latest motherboard and/or chipset on the market, particularly when it's a motherboard manufacturer's first outing with that particular chipset. Why not let others have the headaches and plump for an almost-but-not-quite-spanking-new chipset where early teething troubles will have come to light and (hopefully) been remedied at source?

AMD chipsets

As we mentioned, AMD differs from Intel in not making many of its own chipsets. Life is also complicated by the fact that the latest AMD Athlon processors, namely the Athlon 64 and 64FX, have the memory controller built into the chip itself. This sounds like gobbledegook but it means that the motherboard doesn't need to go through the Northbridge chipset to 'talk' to memory. It does this directly and very efficiently.

The processor does still link to a chipset, which is responsible for handling the video and expansion card buses, drive interfaces, plus integrated audio, networking and so forth, but this connection is not strictly speaking a front side bus. Rather, AMD 64 processors use a different technology which goes by the name of HyperTransport (see **www.hypertransport.org** for details).

What it all boils down to is the fact that making direct comparisons between AMD and Intel motherboards is notoriously complicated, particularly if you focus on chipset specifications alone. Just to reiterate the point, with Athlon 64 processors the two most important buses on the motherboard – those that we usually call FSB (processor to chipset) and memory bus (chipset to memory) – are integrated within the processor and its socket, not provided by the chipset.

That's one significant difference. Another is that AMD chipsets do not currently support DDR2 memory (although they can offer dual-channel performance for DDR). See p.46 for more on this, including why or if it matters.

All of that aside, motherboards built for AMD processors offer much the same in terms of inputs and outputs, support for PCI Express and SATA, integrated audio and graphics ... and everything else. Here is a glance at three current chipsets for the

Athlon 64 processor. By stripping out FSB and memory buses, you'll see that the end result is markedly similar to those Intel models already examined. What that means, ultimately, is that a motherboard for an AMD Athlon is likely to look and behave very much like a motherboard for an Intel Pentium, despite major differences at the structural level.

	Nvidia nForce 4 Ultra	VIA K8T890	SiS 756
PCI slots	6	6	6
PCI Express 16x-speed (for video card)	1	1	1
PCI Express	4	4	2
AGP slot	-		-
IDE sockets	2	2	2
SATA sockets	4	4	4
Integrated audio	Yes	Yes	Yes
Integrated graphics	-	-	-
Integrated LAN	Yes	Yes	Yes

Chipset conundrums

If you're thinking about building a Pentium-based PC, choosing a motherboard would seem to be straightforward: just find the right Intel chipset and all else follows from that. For full details of the entire range, see **www.intel.com/products/chipsets**. If you want an AMD Athlon system, you have to delve a little deeper to find out what memory support is on offer. This means looking not just at the chipset specification in isolation but also at the finished motherboard.

But in fact that's what you should do anyway, even with a Pentium system. The reason is that not every manufacturer implements every aspect of a chipset's capabilities on every motherboard model. On seemingly identical and similarly priced motherboards from different manufacturers, you may find that one has four PCI slots and one has six. How many USB ports do you get – two, four, six or more? Is there a digital output for relaying audio to an external recording device? Two, three or four memory slots? A spare fan connector in case you want to try your hand at over-clocking? A secondary BIOS for emergency use? One or more LAN ports for easy networking? Wireless networking too? Is there an antivirus program, or any other software, thrown in? The list goes on and on. Even within their own ranges, motherboard manufacturers like to baffle us with minuscule differences between one model and the next.

The upshot is that you can narrow down your search to a particular processor, memory type, chipset and even to a particular motherboard manufacturer but *still* have to wade through specification sheets galore. There's no real shortcut, we're afraid, but the trick is twofold: on one hand, make sure you understand what the specifications are telling you; and on the other, have a clear grasp of what kind of computer you want to create. Put the two together and picking a suitable motherboard becomes very much simpler.

A rather stylised view of HyperTransport from the HyperTransport Consortium. Athlon 64 processors include a memory controller in the chip, which means that the processor itself – not the chipset – handles the flow of data between the processor and RAM.

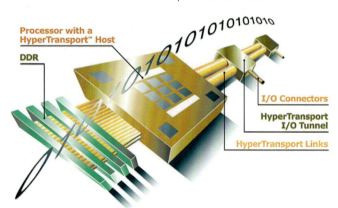

Processor with a HyperTransport™ Host
DDR
I/O Connectors
HyperTransport I/O Tunnel
HyperTransport Links

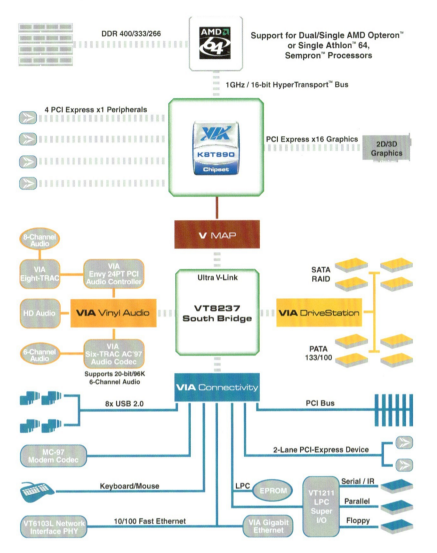

Here are the VIA K8T890 and SiS 756 in all their block-diagram glory. Note again how the memory bus connects directly to the processor, not to the chipset.

SiS756/ SiS965 System Architecture

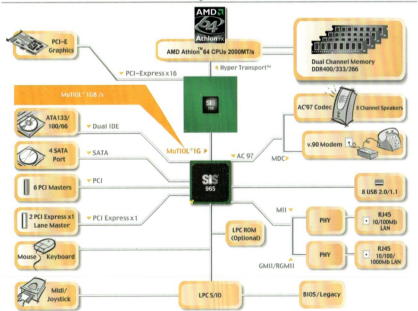

PART 2 Processor

The processor, or central processing unit (CPU), is your computer's 'brain'. It processes data at a phenomenal work rate and largely, but by no means solely, governs the overall performance of your PC. It is also the headline figure in most computer adverts, flagged up with a healthy dose of hyperbole:

Blistering Speeds!
Unbelievable Performance!!
The Fastest Processor In The World ... EVER!!!

You know the kind of thing. But the ads have a point, do they not? If you're building a new computer, surely you need the very fastest chip on the block?

Speeds

In a word, no – or, at least, not unless you have very deep pockets indeed. Intel and AMD are the two main players in the processor market these days and both charge a remarkably hefty premium for the very latest models. The flipside of this equation is that earlier models attract a very healthy discount.

Here, for instance, are Intel's Pentium 4 prices on one random day. Note that these are trade prices based on boxes of 1,000 at a time i.e. the price that an OEM would pay:

Pentium 4 Extreme Edition (GHz)	Price ($)
3.73	999
3.40	999
3.20	925

Pentium 4 (GHz)	Price ($)
3.80	637
3.60	605
3.40	401
3.20	273
3.00	224

Here are AMD's OEM prices on the same day:

Athlon 64 FX model	Price ($)
4000+	643
3800+	424
3700+	329
3500+	272
3400+	223
3200+	194
3000+	149
2800+	122

The actual prices are irrelevant – but just look at the differentials! A 3GHz Pentium 4 processor costs about a third of the price of a 3.80GHz model. What you have to ask yourself is whether you would actually notice the difference between, say, three billion clock cycles per second and four billion. In most cases – that is, short of running an incredibly processor-intensive application such as real-time video-editing software – you simply wouldn't. Besides, is a 25% increase in performance really worth a 330% price premium? Remember too that you can always upgrade to a faster processor later when the price has fallen to a more realistic level. That 3.80GHz chip will cost $200 some day soon.

You won't get far without a processor under the hood. Here we look at the options from Intel and AMD.

Processor evolution

The history of CPUs is long, complicated and dull. Rather than discuss it at any great length, instead we present you with the first of a few tables. This one covers the older Pentium 4 and Athlon XP processors (which can still be obtained if you shop around and can still make very powerful PCs).

Pentium 4	Clock speed[1] (GHz)	L2 Cache[2] (MB)	FSB (MHz)	Socket
3.4	3.40	0.5/1	800	Socket 478
3.20	3.20	0.5/1	800	Socket 478
3	3.06	0.5/1	533/800	Socket 478
2.8	2.80	0.5	533	Socket 478
2.66	2.66	0.5	533	Socket 478
2.6	2.60	0.5	400	Socket 478
2.53	2.53	0.5	533	Socket 478
2.5	2.50	0.5	400	Socket 478
2.4/2.4B[3]	2.40	0.5	400/533	Socket 478
2.26	2.26	0.5	533	Socket 478
2.2	2.20	0.5	400	Socket 478
2.0/2.0A[4]	2.00	0.25/0.5	400	Socket 423/478
1.9	1.90	0.25	400	Socket 423/478
1.8/1.8A	1.80	0.25/0.5	400	Socket 423/478
1.7	1.70	0.25	400	Socket 423/478
1.6/1.6A	1.60	0.25	400	Socket 423/478
1.5	1.50	0.25	400	Socket 423/478
1.4	1.40	0.25	400	Socket 423/478

[1] **Clock speed** is a measure of a processor's work rate, expressed in millions (MHz) or billions (GHz) of cycles per second. Basically, the higher the clock speed, the more instructions a processor can carry out every second. However, the FSB and other key components in a computer system, notably memory, also affect how a processor performs in the real world. Clock speed is thus a guide to overall potential but by no means the end of the story.

[2] **Level 2 cache** is a slither of extremely fast memory integrated within the processor. It acts as a buffer between the chipset and the processor and feeds the latter information at an extremely quick pace. The more the merrier.

[3] The 2.4GHz Pentium 4 is available with an optional 'B' suffix. This tells you that you're getting a processor with a fast 533MHz FSB rather than the same chip with a slower 400MHz bus.

[4] Three Pentium 4 processors are available with an optional 'A' suffix, which tells you that they use Intel's smaller and more efficient 0.13-micron internal architecture (code-named Northwood) rather than the larger, less efficient 0.18-micron architecture (code-named Willamette). If opting for a 1.6, 1.8 or 2.0GHz processor, be sure to get an A model. All Pentium 4s from the 2.2GHz and beyond are Northwoods so the suffix has been dropped because there is no room for confusion.

Athlon XP	Clock speed (GHz)	L2 Cache (MB)	FSB (MHz)	Socket
3000+ (Barton)	2.17	0.5	333	Socket A
2800+ (Barton)	2.08	0.5	333	Socket A
2700+	2.17	0.25	333	Socket A
2600+	2.08	0.25	333	Socket A
2500+ (Barton)	1.83	0.5	333	Socket A
2400+	2.00	0.25	266	Socket A
2200+	1.80	0.25	266	Socket A
2100+	1.73	0.25	266	Socket A
2000+	1.67	0.25	266	Socket A
1900+	1.60	0.25	266	Socket A
1800+	1.53	0.25	266	Socket A
1700+	1.47	0.25	266	Socket A
1600+	1.40	0.25	266	Socket A
1500+	1.33	0.25	266	Socket A

An AMD Athlon XP is slightly cheaper than a comparable Pentium 4, but it's certainly no slouch and certainly not a compromise. Rather, it's just a different building block.

AMD labelling is nothing if not contentious. Athlon XPs have a physically different structure to Pentium 4s and AMD has long maintained that clock speed alone is not a true measure of a processor's potential. Thus it now brands each product with a '+' figure that relates to how it stacks up against a Pentium 4 with a similar clock speed. In other words, an Athlon XP 2400+ is reckoned to be broadly equivalent to a 2.4GHz Pentium 4 despite having a clock speed of only 2GHz. Independent testing backs AMD's assertion, so we won't quibble.

Athlon XPs come with three different core architectures, known as Palomino, Thoroughbred and, most recently, Barton. What's interesting is that the first crop of Barton chips – 2500+, 2800+ and 3000+ – are rated faster by AMD than Thoroughbred chips running at higher clock speeds. The Barton-built 2500+ Athlon XP, for instance, has a clock speed of only 1.83GHz compared with a Thoroughbred 2400+ running at 2GHz. The difference is in the cache: Barton processors have twice that of Thoroughbreds.

'Tis a thing of rare and fragile beauty, is it not? OK, it's not really, but the Pentium 4 is Intel's current front-runner.

? QUICK Q&A
I thought some processors used slots on the motherboard instead of sockets?
They certainly used to but no longer. Intel and AMD have both settled on a more efficient socket approach. Not that their processors use the same sockets, of course; that would be just too easy.

Ringing the changes

To cut to the chase, you are almost certainly going to want to install an Intel Pentium 4 or an AMD Athlon processor in your desktop computer. However, both Intel and AMD have made significant changes to their desktop processors in recent years.

Let's bring ourselves up to date, looking at Intel's moves first.

Pentium 4

It used to be easy to rate a Pentium 4 processor just by glancing at the clock speed. A 3GHz chip was faster than a 2GHz chip and, consequently, more desirable and more expensive. However, Intel now takes the view that the 'sum of the features is greater than GHz alone', to quote from the marketing brief. By this, the company means that clock speed alone is not a sufficient guide to a processor's ultimate capability. It remains a necessary indicator, but no longer stands alone. This, of course, is just what AMD has been saying for years.

Intel now classifies processors in families, gives each family member a number, and lists three key elements for each: clock speed, cache and FSB speed. Thus we find, for instance:

Intel Pentium 4 550 (3.4GHz, 1MB, 800MHz)

This tells us that the model number is 550, the clock speed is 3.4GHz, the Level 2 cache is 1MB and the front side bus runs at 800MHz. Sounds straightforward? Hold on just a minute ...

There are two desktop processor families, namely 5xx and 6xx, with the 3xx series reserved for Celerons (see p.41) and the 7xx for mobile processors (chips used in laptops). Within each family, but only within that family, you can make certain deductions based on the processor number. For example, a 550 is superior *in some way* than a 540. It might have a higher clock speed or perhaps a faster FSB. However, according to Intel:

The digits themselves have no inherent meaning, particularly when looking across families e.g. 710 is not 'better' than 510 simply because 7 is greater than 5 from a numerical perspective. The numbers are aligned with different processor families and thus represent different value propositions to the end customer.

Er, right. Moreover:

Processor numbers are also not a measurement of performance. A higher number does not necessarily mean higher performance for any given usage model or any given system configuration ... a higher number does not always equate to higher clock speed, and furthermore, linear increments between processor numbers are not meant to indicate linear feature advancements.

Still with us? You could be forgiven for thinking that Intel has lost the plot completely with its new numbering system for processors.

Now add to this heady mix some further complications. Pentium 4s have for some time been manufactured using a 130-nanometer technology, otherwise known as 0.13 micron. Previously, the architecture was 180-nm/0.18-micron, as commented upon in note 4 on p.35. But the latest Pentium 4s now use an even smaller architecture measured as 90-nm/ 0.9-micron. This is just something to note, as you will see the architecture listed in some specifications.

Some versions of processors are flagged with a 'J' suffix, which means that they include a form of hardware antivirus protection (called 'Execute Disable Bit' or EDB).

This is a Pentium 4 550 but that alone tells you little these days.

You'll also come across the Pentium 4 in its 'Extreme Edition'. This means that the chip has built-in Level 3 cache on top of the standard Level 2 cache. Basically, this boosts the flow of data between the processor and RAM, which theoretically makes the computer faster. The very latest Extreme Edition chips are now being produced with a 1,066MHz FSB. Annoyingly, and illogically, the Extreme Edition family is not numbered. As of now, Extreme Edition Pentium 4s are strictly for power-hungry gamers with very deep pockets.

Finally, the 6xx series (pus the Extreme Edition 3.73GHz) includes support for 64-bit applications, bringing Intel's processors up to speed with AMD's Athlon 64 range (see p.39–40).

Time for another table. To get the hang of what Intel is trying to tell us, note that the 570, for instance, has a faster clock speed than any processor in the 6xx family. However, all 6xx processors have twice as much Level 2 cache as that found in the 5xx series and cache is important. So, you might wonder, which would perform better: the 570 with its 3.8GHz clock and 1MB of cache or the slower 660 with double the cache?

Intel isn't saying but take it from us that you won't see more than 3–5% difference between the two in any real-world application i.e. when doing stuff on your computer.

Pentium 4	Clock speed (GHz)	Level 2 cache (MB)	FSB (MHz)	Socket
660	3.6	2	800	775
650	3.4	2	800	775
640	3.2	2	800	775
630	3.0	2	800	775
570[1]	3.8	1	800	775
560[1]	3.6	1	800	775
550[1]	3.4	1	800	775
540[1]	3.2	1	800	775
530[1]	3.0	1	800	775
520[1]	2.8	1	800	775
Pentium 4 Extreme Edition	**Clock speed (GHz)**	**Level 2/ Level 3 cache (MB)**	**FSB (MHz)**	**Socket**
	3.73	2/0	1,066	775
	3.46	0.5/2	1,066	775
	3.4	0.5/2	800	775

[1] This processor is available in J and non-J formats.

TECHIE CORNER

Hyper-threading, or HT technology, is a feature that you'll find in all of the Pentium 4 processors listed in this table. Essentially, it enables the chip to process multiple tasks simultaneously rather than sequentially. The result, Intel alleges, is a significant boost in performance during intensive multitasking, almost akin to having a second processor in your system. Indeed, HT specifically seeks to emulate the dual-processor environment that you might see in a top-end system designed to handle sustained number-crunching.

To see the benefits, you need both an HT-capable Pentium 4 processor and a chipset and BIOS that support the technology. Any Socket 775 motherboard will do the business. However, the real-world benefits will vary according to what kind of software you use and even which particular programs.

Hyper-Threading: the poor man's answer to a dual-processor motherboard.

Dual processors. If HT technology apes the power of having two processors working in parallel, how about the real deal? Well, the buzzword here is Symmetrical Multi-Processing (SMP), which means running two or more processors on the same task at the same time in order to complete that task more quickly.

The first thing to say is that standard Pentium 4s don't support dual processing, so you'd need to invest in a pair of server-level Xeon chips and a compatible dual-socket motherboard in which to install them. Athlons are similarly unsuited to dual processing so AMD devotees would need to use Opteron chips. Like the Xeon, these are designed – and priced – for server work.

However, the real problem with SMP, other than the crippling expense of building a Xeon or an Opteron-based system, is that it only works well when used with software that has been written specifically with multi-threading in mind. Most applications are still single-threaded, so running them on a dual-processor system yields precious little benefits. This will doubtless change but for now a dual-processor system is not a particularly attractive proposition for most of us.

Dual-core processors. As if hyper-threading and dual processors weren't confusing enough, you now need to factor in dual-core processors. A dual-core processor is effectively two processors in one chip. As with HT technology, the idea is to allow two independent threads of processing to run in parallel simultaneously; but unlike HT Technology, a dual-core processor achieves this by having two physically discrete processing threads, or channels. Nor will it stop there: both Intel and AMD are committed to multi-core processors with four or eight processing threads per chip. The first dual-core processors will be on the market in mid-2005 (maybe).

Athlon 64

AMD's major change has been a move beyond the long-standing Athlon XP platform, which was itself an enhancement over the plain Athlon design, towards the all-new Athlon 64 and 64 FX.
Here's what you need to know:

● As already noted, AMD numbers its processors in accordance with how they compare in the real world to Pentium 4s. This was and remains a marketing angle intended to overcome buyer resistance to lower clock speeds. This trend continues today, although Intel's move away from selling chips on clock speed alone makes such comparisons increasingly redundant.

● The architecture of an Athlon processor is significantly different to that of a Pentium. In particular, and as already noted, Athlon 64s have the memory controller built into the chip, which means they don't need to rely upon the motherboard chipset for communication between the processor and RAM.

● The FSB is also structured differently, using HyperTransport technology. This provides a far greater bus bandwidth than you'll find on a Pentium 4-compatible motherboard. This equates to faster performance.

● Athlon processors are cheaper than Pentiums. This means that an Athlon-based system usually costs less to buy from a shop and less for you to build. The saving may not be tremendous, but it's real and attractive.

● Like Intel's 'J'-badged Pentium 4s, all Athlon 64s have built-in antivirus protection in the form of Enhanced Virus Protection (EVP). It's no big deal, really – you'll still need to use antivirus software – but it's a welcome last-ditch line of defence. You'll need to install Windows XP with Service Pack 2 for it to work at all.

● The 64 in an Athlon's name is a reference to its ability to execute instructions in 64-bit mode. A 32-bit processor, such

The Athlon 64 is a worthy competitor to the Pentium 4.

as a Pentium 4 or an Athlon XP, can process 2^{32} individual blocks of information per clock cycle. Each block is in fact a byte, or a group of 8 bits, so this equates to 4.3 billion bytes, or 4GB. This in turn determines the maximum amount of RAM that the chip can address: any more RAM would simply be superfluous. However, a 64-bit processor can process 2^{64} bytes per clock cycle. In simplistic terms, this means it can handle many, many more instructions per second and work hand-in-hand with far greater quantities of RAM, thereby potentially improving system performance dramatically. Which would be fine if your system performance needed dramatic improvement. The great limiting factor right now is the lack of operating system and application support for 64-bit processors. Installing a 64-bit processor is like driving a Ferrari in a car park. However, a 64-bit version of Windows is on the cards, at which point software developers will doubtless flock to release 64-bit versions of their programs, so installing a 64-bit processor now is a smart move. Meanwhile, you can of course run any 32-bit software, including Windows, with an Athlon 64.

● The FX part of an Athlon 64 FX's moniker denotes that you're dealing with a special breed of Athlon specially optimised for game play by means of some additional Level 2 cache. Unless gaming is your thing, you don't need to bother with this.

When it comes to raw performance, the difference between comparable Pentium 4 and Athlon 64 processors is negligible in most circumstances. True, if you study sufficient benchmark tests in geeky magazines you may glean that a Pentium 4 is fractionally better suited to task A when conditions B and C pertain; but then you have to balance this with the knowledge that an Athlon can outperform a Pentium at task D when factors E and F hold true.

And none of it matters a jot. Either will suit you perfectly.

Here comes a table. Note the difference between, for example, the Athlon 64 3800+ and the Athlon 64 FX-53. They run at the same clock speed and have the same bus bandwidth, but the FX version has double the Level 2 cache.

Athlon 64	Clock speed (GHz)	Level 2 cache (MB)	HyperTransport processor bus (MHz)	Socket
4000+	2.4	1	2,000	939
3800+	2.4	0.5	2,000	939
3700+	2.4	1	1,600	754
3500+	2.2	0.5	2,000	939
3400+	2.0	1	1,600	754
3200+	2.0	1	1,600	754
3200+	2.0	0.5	2,000	939
3000+	2.0	0.5	1,600	754
3000+	1.8	0.5	2,000	939
Athlon 64 FX	**Clock speed (GHz)**	**Level 2 cache (MB)**	**HyperTransport processor bus (MHz)**	**Socket**
FX-55	2.6	1	2,000	939
FX-53	2.4	1	2,000	939
FX-51	2.2	1	2,000	939

Spot the difference? A Celeron looks just like a Pentium 4 but carries a little less cache.

Budget buyers

You don't have to buy a state-of-the-art Pentium 4 or an Athlon 64. For one thing, you could snap up an older Pentium 4 or Athlon XP and (providing you can source a compatible motherboard with the right socket – and, for that matter, compatible memory) build a perfectly powerful, fast and reliable PC for a fraction of the cost.

Alternatively, consider Intel's and AMD's own second-league ranges, called the Celeron D and the Sempron (formerly Duron) respectively. A Celeron D is essentially a Pentium 4 with some of the Level 2 cache stripped out and a Sempron is basically a rebranded Athlon XP. No HyperTransport bus, integrated memory controller or 64-bit performance here.

The following table shows current availability.

Celeron D	Clock speed (GHz)	Level 2 cache (MB)	FSB (MHz)	Socket
345[1]	3.06	0.25	533	775/478
340[1]	2.93	0.25	533	775/478
335[1]	2.80	0.25	533	775/478
330[1]	2.66	0.25	533	775/478
325[1]	2.53	0.25	533	775/478
320	2.40	0.25	533	478
315	2.26	0.25	533	478
Sempron	**Clock speed (GHz)**	**Level 2 cache (MB)**	**FSB (MHz)**	**Socket**
3000+	2.0	0.5	333	754/A
2800+	2.0	0.25	333	754/A
2600+	1.83	0.25	333	A
2500+	1.75	0.25	333	A
2400+	1.67	0.25	333	A
2300+	1.58	0.25	333	A
2200+	1.5	0.25	333	A

[1] This processor is available in J and non-J formats (i.e. with or without EDB antivirus protection).

To give you an idea of how much you can save with a Celeron D or a Sempron, here are some prices. Compare and contrast these with the Pentium 4 and Athlon 64 pricing on p.34.

Celeron D	Price ($)
345	117
340	103
335	89

Sempron	Price ($)
3000+	103[1]
2800+	90[1]
2600+	80[1]

[1] This is the retail price for a single boxed processor, not the OEM price based on trays of 1,000.

Cooling

Processors get very, very hot when in use and need to be adequately cooled. This usually involves a heatsink unit with a built-in fan that attaches directly to the processor by means of clips. The heatsink has aluminium fins that dissipate heat generated by the hot core of the processor and the fan cools it with a constant flow of air. Many motherboards also have a secondary heatsink to cool the Northbridge chip.

Without a heatsink, a processor would soon overheat and either shut itself down, if you are lucky, or burn out completely and probably take the motherboard with it.

All retail processors ship with suitable units in the box. Indeed, this is one very good reason to pay a little more for the retail packaging. If you source an OEM processor – i.e. one originally supplied to a computer manufacturer and later resold – you will also have to buy a compatible heatsink/fan. This is no great problem but do be sure to get one rated for the clock speed of your processor. It must also be designed for the appropriate socket i.e. a Socket 775 heatsink won't fit in a Socket 478 motherboard.

We cover the installation of heatsinks in detail later. See also Appendix 1 on quiet PCs.

They come in many shapes and sizes but, stylish or otherwise, a heatsink is an essential accoutrement for a hot CPU.

You have to go back a bit to find a slot-based processor but the second-hand buyer may fancy a high-end Pentium III or Athlon.

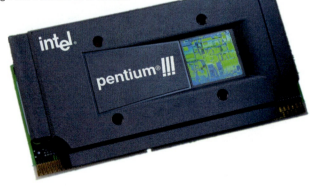

PART 2 Memory

System memory – Random Access Memory (RAM) – is just as critical a component in your new computer as the processor. More so, even. Too little memory and the fastest processor in the world will choke on its workload; stacks of memory and you can run several software applications at the same time without the system stuttering, hanging or crashing.

At the simplest level, computer applications run in RAM, by which we mean the files required to open and maintain a given program are transferred from the hard disk, where the program is installed, to RAM for the duration of the session. If you turn off your computer or it crashes, RAM's memory is 'flushed' or wiped out, so you have to start again. That's why it's so very important to save your work as you go along. Only then are your changes copied from RAM back to the hard drive for permanent storage.

Let's say you want to perform a sum in a spreadsheet. The spreadsheet program isolates the data required to perform the sum. RAM then sends this data to the processor through the Front Side Bus (or in the case of an Athlon 64 processor, directly via the integrated memory controller). The processor crunches the numbers, comes up with an answer, and sends it back to RAM. Finally, RAM feeds the result to your spreadsheet program and the solution appears on your monitor screen.

It all happens very quickly indeed. However, in all but the most intensive applications, such as real-time video editing, the overall speed of the system is governed far more by RAM than by the processor. When a computer runs painfully slowly, chances are that RAM is the bottleneck, not the processor.

Some memory modules sport their very own heatsinks to help diffuse the heat. Cynics argue that these bolt-on accessories are mainly for show, like go-faster stripes.

Modules

RAM comes in the form of chips soldered to long, thin modules that plug into slots on the motherboard. These modules are remarkably easy to install but buying the right modules in the first place is a more complicated matter.

As mentioned above, any motherboard/chipset supports one type of RAM and one alone. This is not to say that you should buy your motherboard first and then look for compatible memory modules as an afterthought. Quite the reverse, in fact: as soon as you've decided between an Intel or an AMD processor, turn your thoughts to RAM and let this decision govern your choice of chipset (and hence motherboard).

Now, we could fill the rest of this manual with techie talk about memory evolution, error-checking, voltages, transistor counts, latency and so forth, but it would make your eyes glaze over and get us almost nowhere. Let's focus instead on the absolute essentials.

DDR-RAM

When the Pentium 4 first appeared, it was 'optimised' for a special kind of proprietary memory licensed (although not actually manufactured) by a company called Rambus. Marketed as Rambus Dynamic RAM, or RD-RAM, the memory modules use a form factor known as RIMM and require corresponding RIMM slots on the motherboard. RIMMs come in 184-pin, 232-pin and 326-pin variations. However, RD-RAM is now almost completely out of favour so we'll say no more about it.

Athlon XP-based systems have always been built around an altogether different type of memory called Double Data Rate Synchronous Dynamic RAM, or DDR SD-RAM (we'll shorten this further to DDR). This comes in modules called DIMMs, which have 184 pins. Again, the motherboard must have compatible DIMM slots. DDR-RAM is manufactured by many different companies and is relatively cheap. The standard has also evolved to keep pace with faster processors and motherboard buses, which basically means that DDR keeps getting faster. It is still the default memory for an Athlon 64 system. A glance at the chipset table on *p X* will tell you that many Pentium 4 motherboards also support DDR modules.

A glance at the chipset table on *p X* will tell you...

QUICK Q&A

How much memory do I really need?

Well, Windows XP supports up to 4GB so that's the practical maximum. Generally, 512MB is about right for fairly demanding work, including audio and video processing, but you'll see real benefits with 1GB under the hood. 256MB suffices for everyday office-style work, web browsing and so forth. Be guided by your software's minimum requirements, but be warned that these are often understated. If a program requires a nominal 64MB, you'll fare better with double that on-board. Much also depends upon how many tasks you run simultaneously on your PC so close down unnecessary programs while using memory-hungry applications.

There are 184 pins in this DDR DIMM. DDR memory is compatible with both Intel and AMD processors.

Doubling up

But that's not the end of the story. The speed of a memory module is rated in a similar way to that for processors. That is, the manner in which it transfers data is determined by a clock. This is really a change in voltage in the memory slot from zero to 2.5V at a given rate, or frequency. A clock speed of, say, 200MHz means the frequency changes 200 million times per second. With each change in frequency, or clock cycle, the memory module can send and receive data. Moreover, DDR memory can send and receive data twice per clock cycle (once on the way up, as the frequency rises from 0 to 2.5V, and once on the way back down again). That's why it's called Double Data Rate.

Beyond DDR we find Dual Double Data Rate RAM (DDR2). This comes in 240-pin modules. The main advantage is that DDR2 operates at higher clock speeds than DDR and transfers data four times per clock cycle rather than DDR's twice. This translates to a higher bandwidth in the sense that more data can pass between RAM and the processor every second. However, DDR2 modules suffer notoriously from high latency. Latency is the delay between an instruction being issued and the instruction taking place. For reasons too dull to explore, the first generations of DDR2 modules had such high internal latencies that they were frequently out-performed in practice by DDR. Only recently have low-latency DDR2 modules begun to turn the theoretical advantage of DDR2 into enhanced performance in the real world. However, as of writing, DDR2 remains the preserve of Pentium 4 chipsets and motherboards. If you build an Athlon-based PC, DDR is the default choice.

DDR2 boosts bandwidth. It comes in 240-pin modules and can only be installed in a motherboard that explicitly supports DDR2 memory.

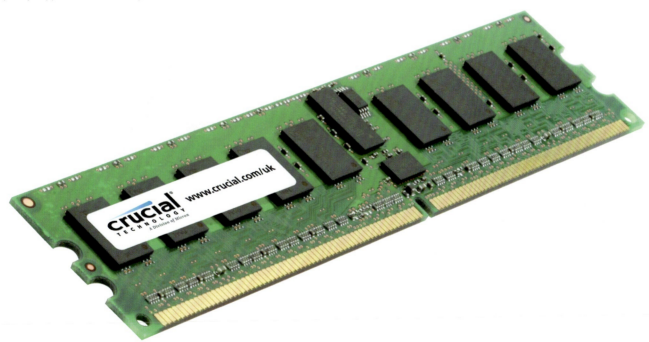

TECHIE CORNER

SD-RAM Before DDR2, DDR and RD-RAM, we had humble Synchronous Dynamic RAM. SD-RAM is dynamic because its contents are flushed continually and lost altogether when you turn off your computer; and it's synchronous because it is synchronised for performance with the motherboard's memory bus. DDR and DDR2 are merely enhancements of this original standard.

Presumably there are still motherboards around that support SD-RAM but only on the second-hand market. Suitable memory modules are also very difficult to obtain. Memory is a commodity market where demand drives supply and there's simply no call for fresh SD-RAM these days. However, it looks likely that DDR will gradually be superseded by DDR2 so, even if you are on an extremely tight budget, we'd strongly advise you to forget about defunct SD-RAM and hang on for a DDR bargain. As with every development in computer generations, the previous, still-powerful generation gets marked down in price very, very quickly. This means that high-bandwidth, high-capacity DDR memory modules will soon be cheap as chips.

You can still get hold of SD-RAM for older motherboards but it's not exactly flying out of Taiwan's fabrication plants these days.

Dual-channel memory

In a nutshell, then, you need DDR memory for an Athlon PC and either DDR or DDR2 for a Pentium 4 machine ... unless, as seems very likely, Athlon chipsets support DDR2 by the time you read this.

Ah, but there's yet another factor at play here. Many motherboards support dual-channel memory configurations. The idea is that you can run two modules in parallel at the same time to effectively double the bandwidth between RAM and the processor. The trick is having two memory controllers on the motherboard.

The standard analogy for dual-channel memory is a jammed motorway. Let's say you have three lanes of traffic cruising at 70mph. If you want to get more cars from A to B in a given time, what can you do? Well, first you can increase the traffic flow by raising the speed limit. This is akin to running memory at ever-faster clock speeds. So now you have a three-lane motorway with traffic hurtling along at 140mph. The next option is squeezing more cars into the available space. This is DDR2's approach. Traffic moves at the same speed – 70mph – but now there's twice as much of it. However, the motorway is now running at full speed with no spare room (or safe distance) between the vehicles. What else can you do to shift more traffic?

You can build an identical motorway alongside the first. This is what a dual-channel memory configuration does. Apply the methodology to a motherboard and in theory it shifts twice as much data to the processor and thus does everything twice as quickly. In practice, the benefits are more modest but it's still an increased performance that you can *feel* rather than merely chart in a benchmark test.

The critical thing about dual-channelling is that you must use two identical modules and install them in the correct slots. If you try to dual-channel with modules of different speeds or capacity it will not work.

The Socket 939 design for Athlon 64 processors supports dual-channelling, as does Socket 775 for the Pentium 4.

Bus bandwidths revisited

Of course, there's little point in sending six lanes of high-speed traffic towards a two-lane roundabout. The bottleneck would be horrendous. In a perfect world of perfect motherboards, the bandwidth of the memory bus and the processor bus (FSB) would match perfectly.

Cast your mind back to p.27 and remember that the bandwidth of a bus is determined by an equation:

Clock speed (MHz) x data quantity (bits) x multipliers

DDR and DDR2 RAM have a 64-bit bus width so each unit of data comprises 64 bits (or, if you prefer, 8 bytes). The multiplier relates first to how many times per clock cycle data is transferred. With DDR memory, the multiplier is two; with DDR2, it is four.

So, for instance, what's the bandwidth of a DDR memory module with an internal clock speed of 100MHz?

100,000,000 x 64 x 2 = 1,600MB/sec

(Divide the answer by 8, to convert bits to bytes, and then by 1,000,000, to convert bytes to megabytes).

If you installed two such modules in a dual-channel configuration, you would double the bandwidth to 3,200MB/sec. This perfectly matches the bandwidth of a Pentium 4 processor with a 400MHz FSB (as shown in the table on p.27). That is, the processor and RAM can share data at 3,200MB/sec with no bottlenecks.

You would see this kind of memory module described in a shop as PC1600 or DDR-200, or usually as both:

PC1600 DDR-200

The PC figure tells you the overall bandwidth in terms of MB/sec; the DDR figure reflects the *effective* speed of the memory bus, which is simply the clock speed times the multiplier. In this example, the memory module's true clock speed is 100MHz but this bus runs at 200MHz thanks to double data rate performance.

The DDR figure is the more important one because this tells you at a glance which type of memory is compatible with your motherboard. For instance, when you see a chipset or motherboard that supports 400MHz memory, you know you need DDR-400 modules.

Still, it's all terribly confusing. In fact, it gets worse when you consider DDR2 memory. Because DDR2 transfers data four times per clock cycle rather than twice, you would expect that a DDR2 module with the same clock speed as a DDR module would have twice the bandwidth. In fact, DDR2 runs with slower clock speeds so it all balances out.

For example, the bandwidth of a DDR2 module with a 100MHz internal clock speed is:

100,000,000 x 64 x 4 = 3,200MB/sec

This module would be advertised as:

PC3200 DDR2-400

The real advantage of DDR2 is that the higher multiplier makes it possible to boost the bandwidth without dramatically increasing the clock speed. DDR2 modules also run at a lower voltage than DDR – 1.8V compared to 2.5V – and consequently generate less heat.

Here's a summary of the current possibilities:

Memory name	Internal clock speed (MHz)	Data transfers per cycle	External memory bus speed (MHz)	Bus width (bits)	Bandwidth (MB/sec)
PC1600 DDR-200	100	2	200	64	1,600
PC2100 DDR-266	133	2	266	64	2,100
PC2700 DDR-333	167	2	333	64	2,700
PC 3200 DDR-400	200	2	400	64	3,200
PC3700 DDR-466	233	2	466	64	3,700
PC4000 DDR-500	250	2	500	64	4,000
PC4300 DDR-533	266	2	533	64	4,300
PC3200 DDR2-400	100	4	400	64	3,200
PC4300 DDR2-533	133	4	533	64	4,300
PC5300 DDR2-667	167	4	667	64	5,300

Selecting memory

The first rule when buying memory is to get the fastest sort that the motherboard supports. That is, if your motherboard chipset supports both 400 and 533MHz buses, spend that little extra on DDR or DDR2 533 modules. If it also supports dual-channel, buy matching pairs and install them in the appropriate slots (see p.88-89). In fact, we highly recommend that you consider only dual-channel motherboards if you want peak performance. Remember, dual-channel uses standard DDR or DDR2 modules so you effectively get twice the performance for no extra outlay. If you take the DDR2 route, consider buying more expensive low latency modules for an extra boost.

Here's another recommendation: don't attempt to match memory modules to motherboards yourself. It's a truly fraught process so make it easy on yourself with an online memory configuration tool. With these, you enter motherboard details at one end and at the other end out pops a list of compatible modules.

Let's jump the gun and test one out.

1

*Crucial Technology's Memory Adviser (**www.crucial.com/uk/index.asp**) invites you to tell it who made your computer, which isn't a very promising start for a DIY system builder. What it really needs to know, of course, are the motherboard details. If you have a motherboard in mind or if you have already bought one, select the manufacturer here. In this example, it is Gigabyte. In the next couple of steps, select your precise model. Choose carefully.*

2

The Memory Adviser helpfully presents a summary of your chosen motherboard's memory support. It's well worth double-checking this against the official specification. Here, for instance, we learn that the motherboard supports up to 4GB (or 4,096MB, which is the same thing) of DDR2 memory in either the PC3200 or PC4300 flavours (a.k.a. DDR2-400 and DDR2-533) in a 240-pin DIMM format. (What Crucial refers to as PC2 4200 appears in our table on p.47 as PC4300. The terms are interchangeable. The additional '2' in PC2 is also optional.)
What this doesn't tell you is whether the motherboard supports dual-channel memory. It does, in fact, but we had to turn to the manufacturer's website for definite confirmation.

3

Here we have a list of compatible modules. Curiously, the most popular purchase is a 1GB PC5300 (DDR2-667) module. This is certainly the fastest module available, which, we'll wager, is why people buy it, but we have just seen that the motherboard supports only PC3200 and PC4300 memory. If you install a PC5300 module, it will simply run at the speed of PC4300. In other words, buying PC5300 memory for this particular motherboard is a complete waste of money (unless you intend to overclock the processor, but that's not something that concerns us here). Which is why it pays to check these things very carefully indeed.

PART 2

Case

Just as all motherboards adhere to certain industry-standard dimensions, so too do computer cases. Far and away the most common form factor is, again, ATX. You can be sure that any ATX motherboard will fit in any ATX case. That's the kind of simplicity that we appreciate. But that's not to say that all cases are the same.

Towers vs desktops

Far from it, in fact. For starters, you can choose between a tower case or a desktop case. One is tall and narrow, the other squat and wide. We heartily recommend going for a tower case. They are overwhelmingly more prevalent than desktop cases and, in our experience, considerably easier to work with. The exception would be if you're building a home-entertainment-style PC for living room use. In this case, style matters almost as much as function.

You can get full-sized, mid-sized and mini tower cases, which are progressively shorter versions of the same thing. The sole advantage of a low-rise tower is neatness; the considerable disadvantage is a corresponding lack of expansion possibilities. A mini-tower will typically have two or three 5.25-inch drive bays, a mid-tower between three and five, and a full-tower anywhere up to seven. Given that you will probably install a CD-RW drive and a DVD-ROM drive, a three-bay case still has room for one

Here we see a full tower case with a side panel removed and its front fascia on and off.

Removable drive bay covers

Lights

Port bracket cover

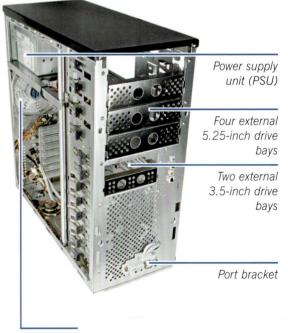

Power supply unit (PSU)

Four external 5.25-inch drive bays

Two external 3.5-inch drive bays

Port bracket

Internal fan

Aluminium cases like this one from Lian-Li are light, strong and cool.

additional device (a sound card breakout box, perhaps) whereas a two-bay case would effectively be full.

Pay attention to 3.5-inch drive bays, too. You'll need at least one for the hard disk drive and another for the floppy drive/card reader. However, we're going to recommend that you install two hard drives and possibly as many as four. Spare internal drive bays thus rank somewhere between desirable and essential.

In short, you want to allow your PC room to grow. Of course, it's always possible to strip the entire innards from a computer and reinstall everything in a larger case should the need arise, but this is about the most drastic and fiddly upgrade you could ever perform. Better, we suggest, to allow for future expansion at the outset.

A non-ATX small form factor platform like this offers little in the way of expansion possibilities, but you may consider that a fair compromise if you need a looker for the living room.

Case features

Drive bays are protected by drive bay covers on the front of the case. These snap-out or unscrew to afford full access to the bay, whereupon you can install an internally-mounted drive.

A case also has a series of blanking plates to the rear that correspond to the motherboard's expansion slots. You'll remove one every time you install an expansion card. Above this is a rectangular input-output (I/O) panel. This is where the mouse, keyboard, parallel, serial and other ports poke through when the motherboard is installed.

On the front of the case, you will find two buttons: the main power on/off switch and a smaller, usually recessed reset button that restarts your computer if Windows hangs. There will be a couple of lights, too: one to show when the power is on and one that flickers whenever the hard disk drive is particularly active. The case may also have an extra opening to accommodate an expansion bracket loaded with audio or USB ports.

Your case may have a single all-encompassing cover that lifts straight off or separate removable side panels. It may be held together with screws, thumbscrews or some arrangement of clips. Internally, you may find a removable motherboard tray. This is a boon, as it's much easier to install the motherboard on an external tray than it is to fiddle around inside the case.

Inside the case, along with the drive bays and a cluster of cables, you'll find a pre-installed fan or two and possibly a mounting area for an optional extra fan. The case will also have a speaker which the BIOS will use to generate beeps (see p.158).

Beyond all of this, designs vary from the standard, boring 'big beige box' look to undeniably funky. Pressed-steel cases are generally cheaper but brushed-aluminium looks (and stays) cooler. Some cases are heavy, reinforced and thoroughly sturdy; others are lightweight, flimsy and easily dented. We would simply advise you to focus on functionality before frills. A full-sized tower case is generally easier to work with, easier to keep tidy internally, more adaptable to customisation and provides better airflow to the motherboard's components.

The same case we saw a moment ago, stripped of its covers and seen from the rear.

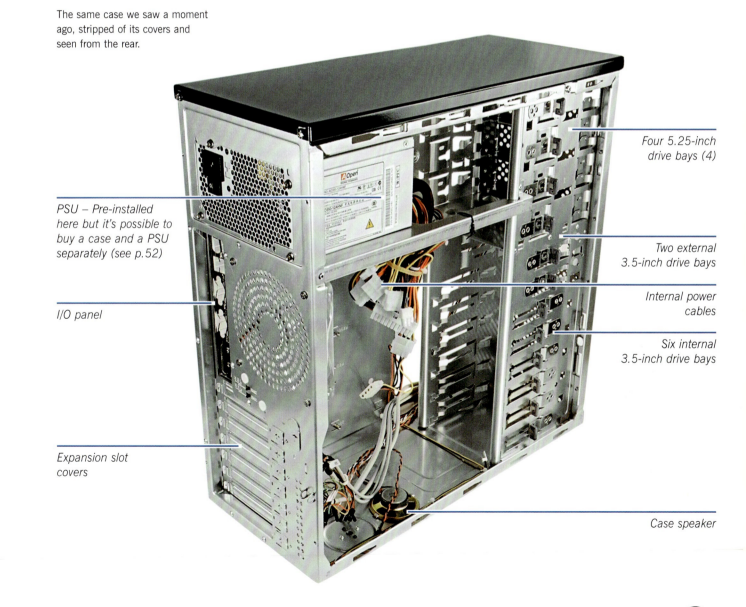

Four 5.25-inch drive bays (4)

PSU – Pre-installed here but it's possible to buy a case and a PSU separately (see p.52)

Two external 3.5-inch drive bays

Internal power cables

I/O panel

Six internal 3.5-inch drive bays

Expansion slot covers

Case speaker

PART  Power supply unit

The power supply unit (PSU) supplies power to the computer's motherboard and drives. That much is obvious. Less so is the importance of getting the right PSU, particularly when many cases come with an anonymous unit pre-installed. Ignore the specifications here and you risk all sorts of problems. If possible, purchase your case and PSU separately, or at least devote as much care to the PSU as to every other component.

Compatibility

To go with your ATX case and ATX motherboard, you need an ATX PSU. Virtually all new PSUs comply with the ATX standard, which means it will fit in an ATX case and power an ATX motherboard.

A reliable power supply unit is a must. This ATX model has an adjustable fan speed for quiet running and pumps out 350W.

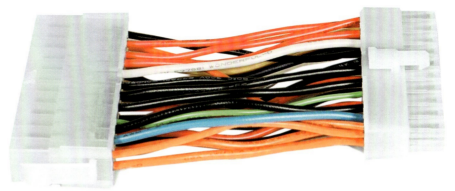

An adapter for converting a 24-pin PSU connector to a 20-pin motherboard.

However, if you are using a Pentium 4 processor and a Socket 775 motherboard, take care. You'll need one of the newer PSUs that has a 24-pin power connector rather than the older 20-pin standard. If you intend to reuse an older PSU or if you buy a 20-pin unit and later find that you can't connect it to our motherboard, all is not lost: you can buy an adapter to convert a 20-pin connector to a 24-pin connector. However, this is not advisable unless the PSU pumps out at least 450W of power. We strongly recommend that you buy a new 24-pin PSU instead. Conversely, though, you can also get an adapter to convert a new 24-pin PSU for use with an older 20-pin motherboard, and that's risk-free.

Also ensure that you get a PSU with SATA connectors if you have a SATA-enabled motherboard and SATA hard drives. Again, an adapter or two can save the day but it is better to buy the appropriate equipment in the first place.

We don't recommend buying a second-hand PSU. An under-powered PSU might not supply power-hungry components with the juice they need, particularly if you cram your case full of drives and accessories, and an older unit with a history of hard work behind it is obviously more liable to burn out and die.

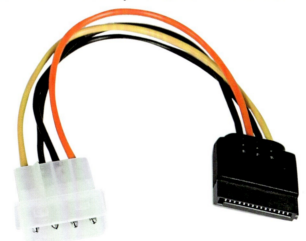

An IDE-to-SATA adapter for powering new-style drives from an older PSU.

Yet another adapter. This one converts a Molex cable into a pair of SATA connectors.

Power rating

A 250W or 300W PSU is inadequate, 350W is fine and 400W is better still. Simple as that.

Cooling

A PSU has an integrated fan that controls airflow through the computer case. Some also have a second fan that blows cool air at the motherboard. We strongly recommend that you buy a PSU specifically rated for a Pentium 4 or Athlon system (whichever applies to you).

Noise

A secondary consideration, certainly, but important nonetheless. Some PSUs make a terrible racket while others operate with barely a whisper. If a peaceful PC is important to you, shop around for a quiet device with adjustable-speed fans. See also Appendix 1.

Connectors

The PSU connects directly to each internal drive in your PC and to the motherboard itself, supplying the lot with power. Here's a run through of what to expect.

TECHIE CORNER

AMD used to be very particular about cooling and airflow requirements on PSUs designed for use with its Athlon XP processors. In particular, it recommended the use of a PSU with an air intake on the bottom of the unit, i.e. in the vicinity of the processor. You can find a list of accredited PSUs at **http://snipurl.com/dlpy**. However, with the move to Athlon 64 and 64 FX, the company is now happy for system builders (like you) to use standard ATX PSUs. That said, dual-fan PSUs are still recommended.

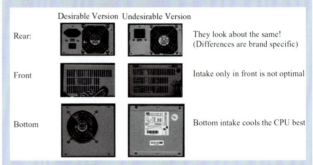

If you're using an Athlon XP processor, don't assume that just any old PSU will do; AMD lays down specific requirements and you'd best buy a unit that abides by them.

ATX power The main power connector that plugs directly into the motherboard. As mentioned above, the design has switched recently from 20-pin plugs to 24-pin.

ATX Auxiliary A secondary 6-pin power connection required by some older motherboards. If your motherboard has an ATX Auxiliary socket, you must connect this cable.

ATX 12V Some Pentium 4 motherboards require yet another cable connection from the PSU to provide extra power to the processor. However, the latest Socket 775 motherboards dispense with this.

Molex drive connector Used to power hard disk and optical drives.

SATA drive connector Used to power Serial ATA hard drives (and some of the latest optical drives).

Berg drive connector Used primarily to power the floppy drive.

PART 2

Hard disk drive

You'll want to install a decent-sized hard disk drive (HDD) in your computer, which means anything upwards of 160GB. Digital video, image and sound files certainly eat heavily into disk space – a single hour of raw footage transferred from a digital camcorder requires a massive 13GB – and you'll find more ways than you thought possible of filling a disk with data. True, you can always add a second or third internal or external HDD later if you run out of room, and non-essential material can also be easily archived on recordable CD or DVD media to free up disk space as and when required, but it's only sensible to start with a sizeable disk from the outset.

The good news is that hard disks are relatively cheap, weighing in at under 50p per gigabyte. However, there are other concerns beyond mere storage.

A hard disk drive stores data on high-speed spinning magnetic platters. Remarkably, they last for tens of thousands of hours.

Interface

The two abbreviations you'll come across most frequently are IDE (Integrated Drive Electronics, sometimes prefixed with an extra E for Enhanced) and ATA (Advanced Technology Attachment). Although technically distinct, these terms are used interchangeably to describe the connection between the HDD and the motherboard.

Another common occurrence is DMA (Direct Memory Access, sometimes prefixed with an extra U for Ultra). This tells you that the device can 'talk' to RAM directly without sending data through the processor first, which is a good thing. And then there's ATAPI, which is ATA with a Packet Interface bolted on. This enables optical CD and DVD drives to use the same interface as the HDD.

For many years, motherboards have come with a pair of IDE/ATA connectors labelled IDE1 and IDE2, each of which can support either one or two devices. IDE1 provides the primary channel, to which you would typically connect the hard disk drive, and IDE2 provides the secondary channel, to which you would typically connect the CD and DVD drives.

However, IDE/ATA is on the way out and in its place we have SATA. The S stands for serial. The slowest SATA bus is wider than the fastest IDE/ATA bus, which means that more data can pass between the drive and the rest of the system per second. See the table below. This, though, is a theoretical enhancement that makes little or no difference to actual performance, for reasons which we'll discuss in a moment. The real difference for system-builders is a new cable design. SATA uses a thin, flexible cable instead of the traditional flat ribbon-style cable, which is both neater and better for airflow around the case.

Interface	Also known as	Maximum bandwidth (MB/sec)
ATA-66	ATA-5, IDE-66 or UDMA-66	66
ATA-100	ATA-6, IDE-100 or UDMA-100	100
ATA-133	ATA-7, IDE-133 or UDMA-133	133
SATA-150	SATA I	150
SATA-300	SATA II	300

Data transfer rates

The real-world performance of a drive doesn't just depend on the bandwidth. In fact, many an ATA-100 drive can outpace an ATA-133 device at reading or saving large files. It comes down to a specification called the internal, or sustained, transfer rate. This is a measure of how quickly a drive can read data from its own disks. The bandwidth figures quoted above relate to the external transfer rate but this merely tells you how quickly the drive can shift data out to the main system. Manufacturers are notoriously reticent about sustained transfer rates, one reason being that the figure is significantly lower than the headline-grabbing external interface.

Sustained transfer rates peak between around 40–70MB/sec, which is some way short of even the ATA-100 standard's external transfer rate, let alone SATA's 150MB/sec and up. The drive may be perfectly capable of pumping out huge volumes of data but this is of questionable value if it can't gather this data at anything like the same rate. The bottleneck is the drive itself, not the interface.

Cables

For an ATA-66 or faster HDD, use only an 80-conductor IDE/ATA cable. This has the same plugs as the older 40-conductor style and looks very similar, but it incorporates twice as many wires within the ribbon. The extra wires are essentially non-functional, but they reduce interference and help preserve a true signal.

Two drives sharing an IDE/ATA channel on the motherboard must be allocated master and slave status in order that the motherboard can tell them apart. This is achieved with little plastic jumpers on the drives. If you mistakenly set both drives to Master or to Slave, neither will work. However, with an 80-conductor cable you can set all drives to the Cable Select position and forget about them: the cable sorts out master/slave status automatically.

With SATA, it's simpler still. This is a one-drive-per-channel technology, which means no more sharing, no more master/slave status, and no more jumpers.

A 40-conductor IDE/ATA cable, an 80-conductor IDE/ATA cable, and a SATA cable.

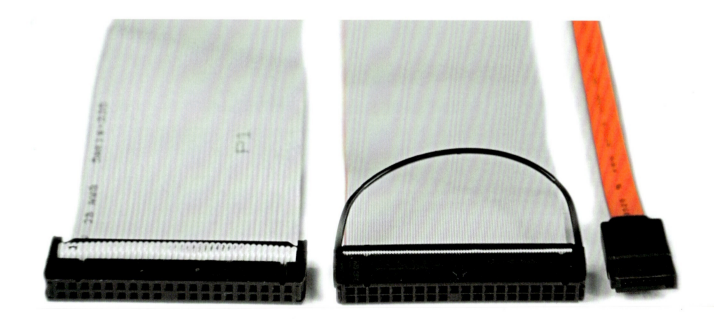

Other considerations

Cache A slice of memory built into the drive that holds frequently accessed data in a buffer state. This saves the drive having to continually re-read from its disks. A 2MB cache is a good minimum; 8MB is desirable.

Spindle speed The rate at which the drive's disks spin. This has a bearing on how quickly the device can read and write data. 5,400rpm is adequate for a low-specification system but we'd recommend a 7,200rpm drive. As a not-entirely-consistent rule, a 7,200rpm drive will have a faster sustained transfer rate than a 5,400rpm drive.

S.M.A.R.T. An error-checking procedure that tries to predict when a hard disk drive is about to fail or, at least, has an increased risk of doing so. This gives you time to make a critical data backup. You need two things: a S.M.A.R.T.-enabled drive and either a motherboard BIOS with native support for S.M.A.R.T. or a standalone software program that works in tandem with the drive.

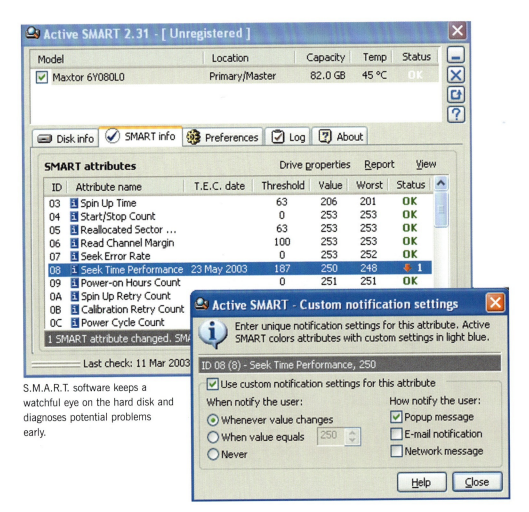

S.M.A.R.T. software keeps a watchful eye on the hard disk and diagnoses potential problems early.

RAID

Once the preserve of network servers, a RAID (Redundant Array of Independent Disks) setup is now a possibility for many home/office computers. Essentially, a RAID-supporting motherboard lets you use two or more hard disk drives simultaneously to 'stripe' or 'mirror' data.

With striping, also called RAID Level 0, the computer treats each hard disk as part of a whole. Two 60GB drives, for example, effectively become a single 120GB drive. Data is then distributed evenly between the drives, resulting in faster read/write performance. The risk is that a single drive failure means all data is lost.

With mirroring, or RAID Level 1, every file you save to the primary hard disk is simultaneously copied to every other drive in the system. Such duplication offers a high level of data security and reliability but, because the additional drives simply mirror the contents of the primary drive, you don't get the benefits of additional storage capacity. It's an expensive way to safeguard your files.

If you reckon RAID is for you, look for a chipset/motherboard with RAID drive controllers and RAID-compatible BIOS. Some motherboards support striping and mirroring simultaneously (Level 0+1), although for this you would need a grand total of four drives.

A RAID adapter expansion card provides additional sockets for connecting hard disks. This is a SATA model. However, an ever-increasing number of motherboards have built-in support for RAID and provide all the sockets you need.

PART 2

CHOOSING YOUR HARDWARE

Sound card

Before buying a sound card, ask yourself four questions:

Do you want to play music on your computer?

Do you want to play games on your computer?

Do you want to watch movies on your computer?

Do you want to record music on your computer?

The answers determine what kind of sound card you need.

A sound card such as Creative Labs Audigy 4 has more bells and whistles built into it than many an entire computer of yesteryear, and even comes with an external input/output box and a remote control. Essential equipment for the musician or gamer but only true audiophiles get really worked up about the nuances of one sound technology over another.

Music

For music playback, be it audio CD tracks, MP3 files or any other format, stereo is usually sufficient. Most music even today is still recorded in stereo so adding a few extra speakers here and there doesn't actually enhance it. That said, some audio hardware and/or software can 'upmix' a stereo signal to give an illusion of surround sound.

Games

Here you'll benefit from a multi-channel surround sound (or 'positional audio') system. This is where the audio signal is composed of several discrete channels relayed to satellite speakers strategically positioned around the listener.

The sound card should also support one or more of the popular sound technologies, including DirectSound3D, THX, A3D and EAX. The trouble is – as you will know if you've ever given this field more than a cursory glance – that there are so many competing, evolving and incompatible standards out there that it's simply impossible to get a sound card that supports everything and to keep up! Still, just about every game will play in a fall-back DirectX mode and should even install the requisite software for you.

Movies

DVD movie soundtracks are almost always encoded in 5.1 or 7.1 surround sound with Dolby Digital or DTS technology. This means you need five or seven satellite speakers plus a subwoofer (for low-frequency tones) to hear the full effect. You also need a sound card that can either decode the signal itself or pass it through to a separate decoder unit that sits between the card and the speakers.

Recording

Should you wish to connect a MIDI keyboard or other controller to your computer, you'll need a MIDI input. This is pretty much standard; most sound cards provide a combined MIDI/games controller port. Look for ASIO support, too. This is a driver standard that reduces the delay, or latency, between, for example, pressing a key on a MIDI keyboard and the sound registering with the recording software. Latency used to make multi-track recording a real pain but ASIO drivers help enormously.

Integrated vs expansion card

But here's the big question: do you need a sound card at all? Many motherboards provide perfectly acceptable, even stunning, multi-channel audio output by means of an embedded audio chip

Fancy a cinema in your sitting room? Then you'll need a multi-channel sound system with speakers to do it justice.

❓ QUICK Q&A

I picked up this old sound card from a stall but it doesn't fit in my PC!
That will be because you were sold an obsolete ISA card and your motherboard has only PCI expansion slots, as is the norm these days. See if you can exchange it for a PCI card.

(which can be a standalone component or part of the main chipset). For instance, look for AC'97 or Realtek ALC880 support.

The traditional disadvantage with integrated audio is that you only get a limited number of inputs and outputs – typically a few on the motherboard's I/O panel and perhaps an optional port bracket – and you may have to fiddle with software settings in order to connect the full array of speakers. However, we have seen more and more motherboard manufacturers wising up to these shortcomings and providing a full array of audio connectors on the I/O panel. Dropping outmoded interfaces like the parallel and serial ports helps to free up space.

Integrated multi-channel audio has advanced to the point where it rivals expansion cards in almost every area. Only the musician or someone with very particular connectivity requirements really need look further.

In any event, we suggest that you select a motherboard with integrated audio and see how it suits. If you decide that you need a separate sound card after all, it's an easy upgrade to perform. Expansion cards always use the PCI interface these days. PCI Express versions will be along shortly but don't be fooled into thinking you need one: sound cards require very little bandwidth so there's no reason whatsoever to splash out on PCI Express when PCI is more than adequate.

When space is tight, sound ports typically double up duties. Two of the three ports here (lower right corner) function either as speaker outputs or as line and mic inputs, depending upon how the audio driver software is currently configured.

PART  **Video card**

Like sound technology, the computer graphics arena is a fast-moving, ever-shifting, highly-competitive minefield of acronyms, abbreviations and indecipherable, incompatible 'standards'. Still, on we go ...

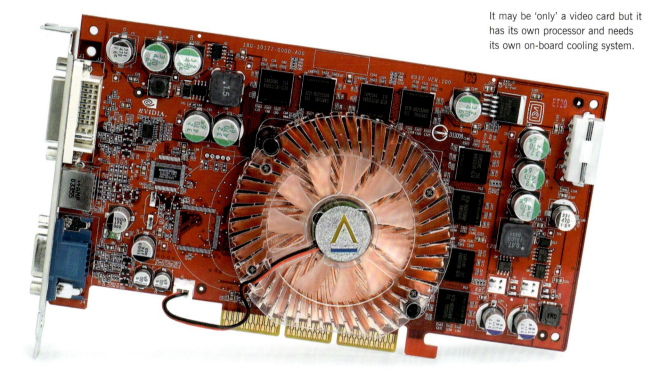

It may be 'only' a video card but it has its own processor and needs its own on-board cooling system.

Chipsets

Just as a motherboard is built around a chipset, so a video card (or graphics card, as they are also called) has at its heart a graphics processing unit (GPU). This is supported by a hefty slice of dedicated RAM located on the card itself. In effect, the video card is like a mini-computer in its own right, albeit with the very specific task of generating images on a monitor screen.

The two main GPU players right now are Nvidia and ATI. Keep an eye on the latest Matrox cards, too, especially if you need multiple monitor support (see Quick Q&A on p.66).

2D/3D

All you need for a two-dimensional display at a comfortable resolution of 1,024 x 768 pixels is a mere 4MB of on-card memory. That's fine for office applications, image editing, web browsing and pretty much everything else. However, computer games demand a lot of additional power. 32MB is about the minimum but you'll find most cards now have 64, 128 or even 256MB of RAM.

3D isn't really three-dimensional, of course, but the card uses complex lighting and texture techniques to create a realistic illusion of depth.

Interface

As we saw earlier, AGP (Accelerated Graphics Port) is a special slot on the motherboard reserved for video cards. At 266MB/sec, the single-speed version has double the bandwidth of PCI; at 8x-speed, it tops 2GB/sec. However, the AGP interface is now rapidly being replaced by PCI Express running at 16x-speed. This provides a massive 8GB/sec of bandwidth, which promises to prove a real (not just a theoretical) advantage for playing fast 3D computer games.

But PCI Express cards don't yet come cheap. Some motherboards have both AGP and PCI Express 16x-speed slots, in which case you can take your pick.

We said earlier that we are reluctant to recommend integrated video unless the motherboard also has a free expansion slot and we reiterate that now. It simply doesn't make sense to rule out future upgrades from the outset. However, if you are sure that 3D isn't your thing, or the children's, or the grandchildren's, a motherboard with an integrated video chip is certainly an economical purchase.

Sitting proudly in its PCI Express slot, this video card boasts up to 8GB of bandwidth – and a truly bizarre cooling system.

DVI

A video card is a natively digital device that has to perform a digital-to-analogue conversion in order to send a signal that an analogue monitor can understand and display. This conversion degrades the integrity of the signal to a degree (a small degree, admittedly). Worse, modern flat-panel TFT monitors are actually digital devices at heart so the analogue signal has to be re-converted back to digital upon receipt. This is patently crazy, hence the evolution of a purely digital connection between video card and monitor: DVI (Digital Visual Interface).

When you connect a DVI monitor to a DVI video card, the digital signal is transferred from one to the other more or less wholesale. The result is a truer image with more faithful colour representations. Better still, there's no need to mess around with fiddly monitor controls in pursuit of a perfect picture: the card and monitor work in harmony to display the best possible image automatically.

The traditional 15-pin VGA plug and socket are disappearing in favour of DVI so a DVI-capable video card is a sensible purchase. If you have an analogue monitor with a VGA cable, a simple adapter will get it connected until such time as you upgrade to a digital display.

If your video card has only one port, make sure that it's DVI. This one has also has VGA, which is handy, but the alternative is a DVI-to-VGA adapter.

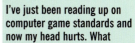

QUICK Q&A

I've just been reading up on computer game standards and now my head hurts. What should I do?

Buy a PlayStation2? Sorry to sound flippant but computer gaming gives us a headache too. With a games console, you know that any game designed for that particular platform – PlayStation, Xbox, GameCube or whatever – will work straight out of the box with no configuration. Which is not to say that we are anti-computer gaming; it's just that we prefer the simplicity of a dedicated gaming platform, just as we'd rather watch a DVD movie on a television screen than a monitor.

This video card ships with a plug-in adapter that provides ports for connecting external video devices.

Optional extras

As well as broadcasting pictures to a monitor, a video card can be put to other uses. These include:

- **TV-out** Hook up your computer to a TV set instead of a monitor to watch movies on the big screen.
- **Video in** Transfer video from an analogue video device such as a VCR or a camcorder onto the hard disk.
- **TV tuner** Connect an aerial and you can watch TV on your PC.
- **Dual-monitor support** Connect two monitors simultaneously for a widescreen effect TV tuner. Plug in an aerial to bring the small screen to your monitor.

For full details of what's possible with a video card and for tests and reviews of all the latest hardware, go to
http://graphics.tomshardware.com/index.html

? QUICK Q&A

My video card has both VGA and DVI ports. Can I connect two monitors?

Probably not. Many video cards provide two outputs but these are mere alternatives i.e. you can use one port or the other but not both simultaneously. If you want to run two monitors, the usual approach is to install a PCI video card alongside the AGP card and connect one monitor to each. Windows recognises this arrangement automatically so configuration is straightforward.

However, you can also get 'dual-head' and 'triple-head' video cards that incorporate all the circuitry required to run two or three monitors through the same bus. This is actually preferable because you get an AGP-generated display on each monitor and it doesn't eat into your allocation of PCI slots.

For the best results with multiple-monitor displays, invest in a specialist card like the Matrox Parhelia. One DVI channel can be split to run two monitors, meaning that up to three can be powered simultaneously from a single AGP interface.

PART 2 Optical drives

The 'average' shop-bought PC these days has two optical drives: a CD-RW drive and a DVD-RW drive. In fact, the rapid uptake in recordable DVD after a shambolic start has been the only significant shift in optical technology recently, to the point where a DVD writer is *de rigueur* and no doubt about it.

Interface

If your motherboard has two IDE/ATA controllers, as is the norm, you can connect two devices to each. Typically you would install the HDD on the motherboard's primary channel (IDE1) and have your CD and DVD drives share the secondary channel (IDE2).

You don't need to use 80-conductor cables with optical drives (see p.57) but it does no harm and gives you the useful option of being able to set the jumpers on both devices to Cable Select.

However, as we have discussed already, the IDE/ATA interface is gradually being phased out in favour of SATA. Although CD and DVD drives have no practical use for the increased bandwidth that SATA provides, it is possible – and indeed sensible – to buy a drive with a SATA socket rather than IDE/ATA. This ensures that you'll be able to reuse the drive in a future PC that uses a SATA-only motherboard. It also saves all that fuss with jumpers and helps keep the inside of your computer case tidy and cool.

To play music on audio CDs or a DVD movie soundtrack through the computer's speakers, you can connect the drive's analogue or digital audio output to one or other of the sound card's audio inputs (or directly to an analogue or digital socket on the motherboard if your motherboard has integrated audio). That said, in virtually every case you can forego this cable completely and allow the computer to extract audio directly and digitally through the IDE/ATA or SATA bus (see p.137).

Looking at a typical drive from a less flattering angle, from left to right we see the digital (small) and analogue (larger) audio cable sockets, the jumper pins, the IDE/ATA ribbon cable socket and finally the 4-pin Molex power socket.

CD and DVD

A plain CD-ROM drive can read and play CDs but a CD-RW drive lets you make your own. There are two types of media: CD-R discs that, once full, can not be erased or re-recorded and CD-RW discs that can be reused time and time again.

To read DVD discs, be they data, audio or movie, you need a DVD-ROM drive. But if you want to make your own DVDs, you need a DVD writer – and that's where the fun begins ...

Recordable DVD

There are three distinct DVD recording technologies around: DVD-R/-RW (the 'dash' or 'minus' formats), DVD+R/+RW (the 'plus' formats) and DVD-RAM. The R stands for recordable, in the sense that you can use a blank disc just once; while RW denotes Rewriteable, which means you can erase a disc and reuse it.

Each format has its pros, its cons, its proponents and its detractors.

● To backup and safeguard your own files, any format will do just fine. You needn't worry about compatibility issues if sharing your discs is not an issue.

● To turn a video file into a DVD movie that you can watch on the DVD player in your living room, check which recordable DVD technology the player can read and buy a drive to match. DVD-R/-RW has the widest drive/player compatibility, DVD+R/+RW runs a close second and DVD-RAM is incompatible with most DVD players. That said, in recognition of recordable DVD's popularity, more and more DVD players are offering support for all formats. This means that compatibility is no longer the burning issue it once was.

● Many DVD drives now also support all recording formats, which means you can throw just about any recordable media at them and emerge with a perfectly playable DVD. A multi-format drive is a smart choice.

Recording/writing/burning (one and the same) your own audio, data and video CDs is a breeze. Windows XP supports basic CD recording without the need for any third-party software.

● So too is a drive that supports dual-layer recording in the +R format. When paired with a dual-layer disc, this increases capacity from 4.7GB to 8.5GB. That equates to more movies or files per disc and, importantly, makes for easier backups. And with a double-sided dual-layer disc, you can go all the way to 17GB per disc.

● All DVD writers can record CDs, too. You may therefore feel that a single drive is all you need in new system. Indeed, if you're building a small form factor PC, one drive is all you'll have room for. The only real disadvantage is that you can't perform direct disc-to-disc copying when you have but the one drive. However, this limitation is not fatal: any decent recording software will extract an 'image' (copy) of the original disc, save it on the hard drive, then copy it onto a blank disc later.

A recordable DVD drive looks just like a CD drive but there's a power of technology packed into that case. This is a dual-layer multi-format model.

Speed

Here's something not to worry about: read and write speeds. All recordable drives carry a cluster of speed ratings which refer to how quickly they burn discs of different formats. The very first generation of CD-ROM drives read data at a top rate of 150KB/sec and faster speeds are expressed as a multiple of this speed: 2x, 4x and so on. For instance, a 40x-speed drive can read data at 6,000KB/sec. Drives are usually slowest at writing data (or recording – it means the same thing) but there's not much in it these days.

DVD-ROM drives are also speed-rated. However, the base speed here is 1,385KB/sec, which is about nine times faster than an original CD drive. A 16x-speed DVD drive thus reads data at a rate of over 21MB/sec. Not that you really need this kind of speed in everyday use; a 1x DVD drive is adequate for movie playback. Again, recording speeds are slower but usually plenty fast enough.

By way of example, here are the speed ratings for the drive we use in our two PC projects later:

Media	Read speed	Write speed
CR-ROM	48x	-
CD-R	48x	48x
CD-RW	48x	24x
DVD-ROM	16x	-
DVD-R	16x	16x
DVD-RW	16x	6x
DVD+R	16x	16x
DVD+RW	16x	8x
DVD+R dual-layer	16x	4x

Buffer under-run protection (or burn-proofing) is built into most CD and DVD writers these days and dramatically reduces the number of spoilt discs they churn out.

PART 2

CHOOSING YOUR HARDWARE

Other possibilities

There's no shortage of potential add-ons and optional extras for a fledgling computer. Here we discuss a few essentials and suggest some other possibilities.

Modem

An obvious must-have for internet access. The current standard for analogue dialup modems – i.e. modems that use a standard telephone line to connect to the internet – is V.92, the successor to V.90. While not actually any faster, the V.92 standard includes a 'modem-on-hold' feature that lets you accept a phone call on the same telephone line without dropping a live internet connection. This, however, only works if your Internet Service Provider actively supports modem-on-hold; a V.92 modem alone is not sufficient.

It's perfectly possible for a motherboard to offer an integrated modem, in which case you'll find an RJ-45 socket on the rear input/output panel, but this can not be taken for granted. A PCI modem expansion card is cheap, reliable and easy to install. Even if you intend to use a broadband internet service, we guarantee that there will be times when the service goes down and you'll be glad of a dialup PCI modem, if only to check your e-mail.

DSL and cable modems are not really modems at all but that's what you need for broadband internet access. Well, that and a broadband service provider.

A DSL or cable modem will generally be supplied as part of any broadband internet deal but you may need to install your own analogue modem for dialup internet access.

Speed Touch USB

ALCATEL

70

Network Interface Card (NIC)

It often makes sense to link computers together in a local area network (LAN). This lets you easily exchange files, share an internet connection and remotely access devices like printers and drives. At its simplest, you can connect two PCs by installing a NIC in each and connecting them with a 'crossover' Category 5 Ethernet cable. To network three or more computers, you need standard non-crossover Category 5 cables with a network hub or switch between them to act as traffic-master. Windows has all the software you need so network configuration is virtually automatic.

When shopping for a NIC, your main choice is between a card that supports Ethernet (or 10BASE-T), Fast Ethernet (100BASE-T), or Gigabit Ethernet (1,000BASE-T). These have theoretical maximum bandwidths of 10Mb/sec, 100Mb/sec and 1,000Mb/sec respectively. Dual- or triple-speed Ethernet PCI cards are commonplace, cheap and ideal.

However, many, probably most, motherboards now provide native support for networking – you'll find an RJ-45 socket or two on the rear input/output panel – and this makes a standalone NIC redundant. Check before you buy.

Wireless networking (Wi-Fi)

If you want to connect PCs without running network cables around your home, install a Wi-Fi adapter. This is essentially Ethernet without wires. There are in fact three main Wi-Fi standards, known as 802.11a, b and g. The oldest of these, 802.11b, runs at a theoretical maximum speed of 11Mb/sec (about the same as the slowest version of Ethernet). This has since been largely replaced by 802.11g, which runs at 54Mb/sec. Hardware designed for either 802.11b or 802.11g will work together smoothly. 802.11a also runs at 54Mb/sec but is considerably less common and is not compatible with the other two standards.

Again, some motherboards provide built-in Wi-Fi.

FireWire (IEEE-1394)

FireWire is a high-speed (50MB/sec) interface particularly suited to transferring digital video from camcorder to computer or for connecting fast external drives. Need we say that FireWire is increasingly supported by motherboards?

It's an Apple trademark but FireWire works just as well on a PC as a Mac. If your motherboard comes up short, install a PCI expansion card.

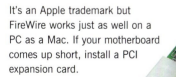

A network interface card is not required when networking capability is provided by the motherboard.

A PCI Wi-Fi adapter gets computers connected at high speeds through the ether.

Killing two birds with one stone: a multi-format memory card reader plus floppy drive.

Media card reader

If you have a digital camera or a PDA (Personal Digital Assistant, or handheld computer), chances are it stores images and other files on a removable memory card. To transfer these files to your PC for editing, you can either connect the device with a cable – usually USB – or else plug the memory card into a card reader. You can get external card reading hardware, which is cumbersome, or internal models, which are convenient – particularly if it doubles-up as a floppy drive.

And the rest ...

A mouse, keyboard and monitor are definite givens, and a printer and scanner are obvious peripherals. But how else might you augment your PC?

Headphones and microphone Listen to music or games and record your own voice – or anything else – with a microphone. Windows has a sound recorder built-in but your sound card's software is likely to be more advanced. For use with speech recognition software, the best bet is a quality headset with an earpiece and microphone combined.

Joystick or games controller. These usually connect via a USB port but you can also get cordless models for greater flexibility.

USB hub Need more USB ports? A hub can add four or more with ease. You can get standalone external boxes or drive-mounted hubs that provide extra ports on the front of your computer.

Games controllers come in all shapes and sizes, from a simple joystick to this (whatever it may be).

This PCI expansion card provides SATA sockets for additional hard drives.

IDE or SATA controller card Add extra channels to your motherboard and connect another couple of hard disk drives. Essential for RAID, unless your motherboard provides native RAID support, and handy for massive storage requirements.

UPS (Uninterruptible Power Supply) Protect your files from power cuts with a UPS. Basically, it's a mini-generator that kicks in when the lights go out.

If the lights go out unexpectedly, will your data go with them? Not if you invest in a UPS.

Bluetooth A Bluetooth adapter lets your computer 'talk' to and exchange files wirelessly with other Bluetooth-enabled devices, notably mobile phones and PDAs.

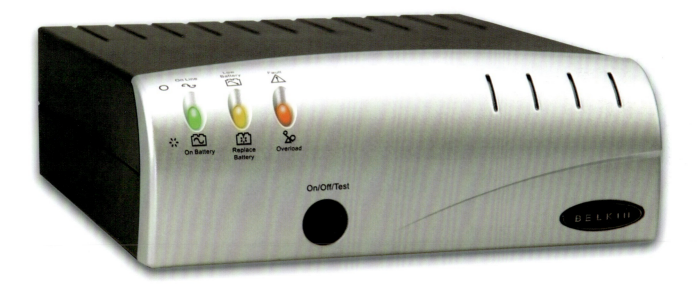

PART 2 **The perfect PC**

We're going to build two computers from scratch: one that uses bang-up-to-date components in a standard tower case and a small form factor PC for gaming or home entertainment.

Making choices

The basic decision-making process looks like this:
- **Pick your processor** A Pentium 4 or Athlon 64 packs a lot of power; a Celeron D or a Sempron is a good compromise if you don't intend to stretch your hardware.
- **Choose your memory** For a Pentium 4, the obvious choice is DDR2; for an Athlon, it's currently DDR.
- **Integrated multimedia** Decide whether you want on-board sound and video or separate expansion cards.
- **Form factor** ATX and a tower case will likely do nicely but, as just mentioned, we're also going to build a cute computer.

With these issues settled, you need to find a good motherboard with a chipset that provides all the right features. Sounds simple? Well, it is, more or less. The main factors to consider, check and check again are:
- **Processor support** What socket does the motherboard have? What processor clock speeds does it support? What is the top FSB?
- **Memory support** What type of memory does the motherboard support, and how fast can it run? Is dual-channel an option? How much memory can you install? Are there any important restrictions?
- **Multimedia** What AGP speed is supported? Is there a 16x-speed PCI Express slot instead? Or both? If the motherboard has an integrated video chip, is there also a vacant AGP slot? If the motherboard has an integrated sound chip, does it offer surround sound?
- **Hard disk drive support** Does the motherboard provide IDE/ATA or Serial ATA? Both would be ideal.
- **Inputs and outputs** How many PCI expansion slots does the motherboard provide? How about PCI Express? How many external interfaces/ports are included on the input/output panel – and which ones?

Chipset choices

For the first project, we decided first to build a high-end, powerful but general-purpose Pentium 4-based computer with stacks of expandability. We could as easily have opted for an Athlon 64 but the coin came down heads. Besides, we use an Athlon for the second computer.

Dual-channel DDR2 RAM made sense to make the most of a fat processor, and we were happy with integrated audio (but not with integrated video). At the time of writing, the natural chipset choice for this kind of configuration was one of Intel's 925 or

915 ranges – but which one? Here are the key differences. The only really significant difference is that the 925XE supports the fastest available FSB, which makes it more suitable than the others for a future processor upgrade. On that basis alone, we plumped for the 925XE.

	925XE	925X	915P
FSB (MHz)	1,066/800	800	800/533
Memory support	PC3200 DDR2-400 PC4300 DDR2-533	PC3200 DDR2-400 PC4300 DDR2-533	PC3200 DDR2-400 PC4300 DDR2-533
Dual-channel support	Yes	Yes	Yes
AGP	No	No	No
PCI Express 16x-speed	Yes	Yes	Yes

Motherboard matches

The chipset settled, we could then set about finding a suitable motherboard. This is a turgid business of wading through specification sheets and reviews, so we'll spare you the details and simply say that we eventually decided upon the GA-AENXP-DW from Gigabyte. This is by no means an endorsement of one company's products over any other, but merely a reflection that you have to buy something eventually!

Here is the full specification:

Feature	Specification
Form factor	Full-size ATX (30.5cm x 24.4cm)
Chipset	Intel 925XE
Processor interface	Socket 775 for Pentium 4
FSB (MHz)	1,066/800/533
Memory interface	4 x DDR2 DIMMs with dual-channel support
Memory support	PC3200 DDR2-400/PC4300 DDR2-533
Maximum memory	4GB
Video interface	PCI Express 16x-speed
Integrated audio	Realtek ALC880 codec with 7.1 support
Sound ports	Front channel out, rear channel out, side channel out, centre/subwoofer channel out, line in, mic in, coaxial SPDIF out, coaxial SPDIF in
Expansion slots	3 x PCI Express 1x-speed, 2 x PCI
HDD interface	1 x IDE/ATA-100, 1 x IDE/ATA-133, 2 x SATA II, 8 x SATA I
Floppy controller	Supports 1.44MB drive
Inputs/outputs	1 x parallel port, 2 x PS/2 ports
USB 2.0	4 x ports on input/output panel, 2 x ports on rear bracket
FireWire	2 x ports on rear bracket
LAN	Gigabit Ethernet
Wi-Fi	802.11g
Modem	No
BIOS	Dual BIOS (Award)

繁體中文 | Contact Us | Site Map

Advanced Search

🏠 Home | Company | Products | Support | Awards | News | Where to Buy

Worldwide
Select Languages ▼

Cherish your motherboard manual dearly for it contains many marvels. It will serve you well throughout your project and prove invaluable every time you upgrade, trouble-shoot or maintain your system. If you lose it, download an electronic copy from the manufacturer's website.

Home > Support > Motherboard > Manual > **Manual of GA-8AENXP-DW**

🏆 **Find** What are you looking for?

Get Acrobat® Reader — You will need to view these PDF files with Acrobat Reader.

		GA-8AENXP-DW			
Download	Language	Revision	File Format	Size	Note
💾	English	1001	pdf	9.59 MB	
💾	English	1002	pdf	0.38 MB	Sil3114 SATA (RAID) Manual
💾	Traditional Chinese	1002	pdf	0.58 MB	Sil3114 SATA (RAID) Manual

‹ Back

RTMM

Read The Motherboard Manual before you start and look closely for any errata sheets or special warnings. For instance, you may find that you have to follow certain rules when installing the memory modules. This will certainly be the case in a dual-channel configuration. You may also find an alert about the inadvisability of installing an old AGP video card. The voltage requirement for powering the AGP interface stepped down from 3.3V to 1.5V during the switch from 2x-speed to 4x-speed AGP, so plugging a 2x-speed card into a newer slot won't work and can do damage, even though the card itself physically fits. In short, don't start work until you have understood the motherboard's layout and requirements.

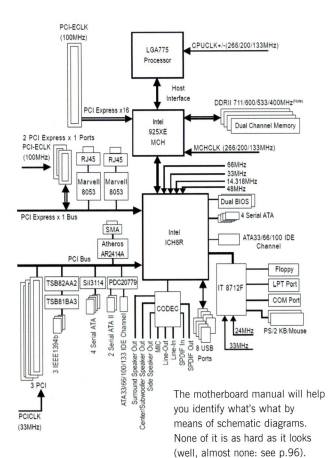

The motherboard manual will help you identify what's what by means of schematic diagrams. None of it is as hard as it looks (well, almost none: see p.96).

GA-8AENXP-D Motherboard Layout

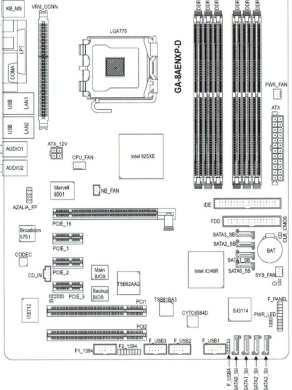

The moral of which is ...

Buy your motherboard and read the manual thoroughly before shopping for other key components! You might even download the manual before making a purchase, particularly if you intend to reuse salvaged components and need to rule out incompatibilities. There's nothing worse than having a heap of useless hardware on your hands for want of checking the specifications – and yes, that is a note of bitter experience.

In fact, precisely because of such hidden but critical details, we strongly suggest that you split your component shopping into three stages, punctuated with a bout of manual reading:

- Buy your motherboard.
- Buy your processor, memory, case and PSU.
- Buy everything else.

The perfect PC Mark I

Finally, here is the full complement of components that we use in the first of our projects. Your hardware and suppliers may well be very different but it's a useful reference point nevertheless.

Component	Manufacturer	Model/specifications	Notes
Motherboard	Gigabyte	GA-8AENXP-DW	As just described
Processor	Intel	Pentium 4 550 (3.4GHz, 1MB, 800MHz) with heatsink/fan	A Pentium 4 Extreme Edition would be a better match for our 1,066MHz FSB motherboard but these processors were far beyond our budget. Later, though, when prices fall, a faster processor would make a nice upgrade.
Case	AOpen	A6000A	A mid-size ATX aluminium tower with bags of expansion room, a 12-cm fan and a rather fetching black lacquered finish.
PSU	AOpen	AO350	A 350W unit with a 24-pin power connecter and SATA power cables.
Memory	Crucial Technology	2 x 1GB PC-5300 DDR2-667 modules (part number CT12864AA667)	These will be installed in a dual-channel configuration to provide 2GB of RAM running at effectively double the normal bandwidth. It's worth noting that this memory is actually faster than the system can use to full advantage, because the motherboard supports only up to DDR-5300, not DDR-667. In other words, we've overspent. Oops.
Hard disk drive	Seagate	2 x Barracuda 120GB (7,200rpm)	Two drives give us the option of a RAID setup or an easy backup routine (see p.59 and 142).
Floppy disk drive	Mitsumi	7-in-1 memory card reader and floppy drive	Why settle for a floppy when you can have a memory card reader in the same drive?
DVD drive	Lite-On	Multi-format dual-layer DVD writer	This model handles all recordable formats, including RAM and dual-layer media.
Sound card	-	-	-
Video card	Gigabyte	GV-RX70128D	An extremely powerful bit of kit. This is a PCI Express 16x-speed featuring the ATI RADEON X700 chipset with 128MB of onboard memory and a silent cooling system.

The perfect PC Mark II

For our second project, we wanted to build a home entertainment-style PC based on an Athlon 64 processor. This proved easier said than done, as at the time of writing there was only one Athlon-compatible small form factor (SFF) motherboard available. However, this came in the welcome shape of a Shuttle barebones system.

The idea behind barebones kits is that you get much of the hardware you need in a single box. It's certainly convenient but it's also essential, as SFF kits tend to use non-standard motherboards, proprietary PSUs and custom cooling systems. All you have to do is buy a compatible processor, a couple of memory modules and a drive or two. The model we selected has integrated audio, USB and FireWire and gigabit Ethernet. However, a glance at its diminutive size tells you that there's not a great deal of room for drives or expansion. Here's the full specification:

Feature	Specification
Form factor	Proprietary design for the Shuttle FN95 motherboard
Chipset	nVidia nForce 3 Ultra
Processor interface	Socket 939 for Athlon 64
HyperTransport (MHz)	1,000
Memory interface	2 x DDR DIMMs with dual-channel support
Memory support	PC2100 DDR-266/PC2700 DDR-333/PC3200 DDR-400
Maximum memory	2GB
Video interface	AGP 8x-speed
Integrated audio	Realtek ALC655 codec with 5.1 support
Sound ports	Front channel out, rear channel out, centre/subwoofer channel out, line in, line out, mic in, coaxial SPDIF out, optical SPDIF in, optical SPDIF out
Expansion slots	1 x PCI
HDD interface	2 x IDE/ATA-133, 2 x SATA I
Floppy controller	Supports 1.44MB drive
Inputs/outputs	2 x PS/2 ports
USB 2.0	4 x ports (2 front, 2 rear)
FireWire	2 x ports (1 front, 1 rear)
LAN	Gigabit Ethernet
Wi-Fi	No
Modem	No
BIOS	Award

With so many features included and so little room for expansion, our shopping list for this PC was much reduced. Here are the details.

Component	Manufacturer	Model/specifications	Notes
Barebones kit	Shuttle	SN95G5 XPC	The kit comes with a Socket 939 motherboard that's compatible with Athlon 64 and 64 FX processors. The case is aluminium and comes with a proprietary 240W PSU.
Processor	AMD	Athlon 64 FX 3500+. No need for a heatsink because the Shuttle kit has its own cooling system.	We couldn't resist the FX version with its extra chunk of cache.
Memory	Kingston Technology	2 x 512MB PC-3200 DDR-400 modules (part number KVR400X64C3AK2/512)	These will be installed in a dual-channel configuration to provide 1GB of RAM running at effectively double the normal bandwidth. We chose the fastest memory that the motherboard chipset supports, but not its maximum complement of 2GB.
Hard disk drive	Seagate	1 x Barracuda 120GB (7,200rpm)	As with the Pentium 4 system earlier.
Floppy disk drive	Mitsumi	7-in-1 memory card reader and floppy drive	Also as before.
DVD drive	Lite-On	Multi-format dual-layer DVD writer	And again.
Sound card	-	-	-
Video card	Creative Labs	3D Blaster Ti4200	The motherboard has an 8x-speed AGP slot so we installed an 8x-speed card.
Wi-Fi card	US Robotics	Wireless Turbo PCI Adapter	With no built-in wireless networking, installing a Wi-Fi card is a sound move. However, we could have gone for a USB 'dongle', which would have the advantage of leaving the sole PCI slot clear for a different type of expansion card, such as a TV tuner. A lack of space forces such choices.

All unpacked and raring to go.

3

PART 3 **Putting together a Pentium desktop PC**

Now comes the time to actually assemble your computer
– or, in our case, computers. We'll start with the Pentium
4 tower system. Start early and you could have a new PC
up and running by dinner time. However, you may prefer
to start and stop at strategic intervals so here we break
the construction process down into sensible sessions.

PART 3 All set?

Just time for a couple of last-minute checklists.

Tooling up

There's no need to equip a workshop with expensive gadgets to build a computer. Here is a full and comprehensive list of all you will need.

- **Antistatic mat and wrist-strap** Electrostatic discharge (ESD) can do serious damage to motherboards and expansion cards, so protect your investment. At a minimum, we strongly recommend that you wear an antistatic wrist-strap whenever handling components. This should be clipped onto an unpainted bare metal part of the computer case. Better still, use an antistatic mat as well. In this case, you connect the wrist-strap cable to the mat and then connect the mat itself to the case. A component should be left safely ensconced within the antistatic bag it came in until you are ready to use it, and then rested on the antistatic mat before installation. Always – and we mean always! – unplug the power cable from the computer before commencing work.

Not a soldering iron in sight. You don't need a degree in electronics to fill a computer case with components.

A case full of computer tools is a clear case of overkill for the hobbyist system builder.

- **Screwdrivers** A couple of Phillips and flat-head screwdrivers will suffice.
- **Pliers** Get hold of a pair of plastic pointy pliers or other pick-up implement for setting jumpers and retrieving dropped screws.
- **Air duster** A can of compressed air is more of an ongoing maintenance tool than a construction aid, to be honest, but is useful for de-fluffing and unclogging second-hand components.
- **Adequate lighting** An Anglepoise or similar light is really useful. Ample daylight is a bonus and a small clip-on torch essential.
- **Patience** Tricky to illustrate on the page but an essential component in any successful PC project. It's best to accept from the outset that not everything will run entirely smoothly. We can guarantee that you will drop the odd screw inside the case, for instance, and it's a fair bet that you will hesitate when required to insert a memory module or heatsink with rather more force than seems reasonable. There's also a chance that something relatively minor – a forgotten cable here, a wrongly set jumper there, a loose connection anywhere – will set you back awhile and force a bout of fraught troubleshooting. But throughout the entire procedure, stay relaxed and think logically. Short of a hardware failure in a specific component, which is itself easily diagnosed, rest assured that your efforts will be rewarded.

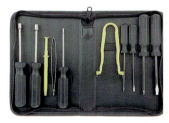

Ready-made screwdriver/pointy-thing kits like this one from Belkin are ideal.

PART

Installing a Pentium 4 processor and cooling unit

The first few steps are more easily accomplished before the motherboard is installed in the system case. Set up your antistatic mat on your work surface, touch something metal to discharge any static electricity that you're already carrying, connect and put on your wrist-strap, and carefully remove the motherboard from its protective bag, holding it only by its edges. Now lay it flat on the mat and behold the marvel of microelectronics.

Note: If your computer case has a removable motherboard tray, remove it from the case now and attach the motherboard to it before going any further. See p.90–93.

This is a Pentium 4 motherboard, and the processor will be installed in a Socket 775. The main difference between this and the previous Socket 478 design is that the pins which connect the processor to the socket are now located in the socket itself rather than on the processor. Unclip and raise the lever that runs alongside the socket.

You can now remove the protective plastic plate and expose the socket pins. Leave the lever in the upright position with the open metal frame raised.

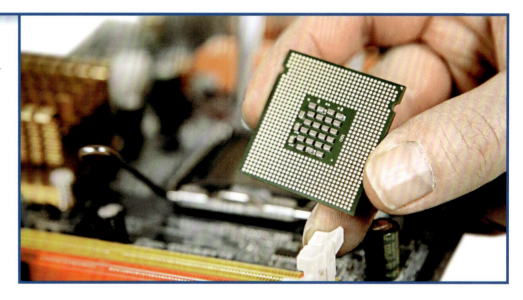

Hold the processor carefully like this, touching only the edges. On the bottom, look for a gold triangle in one corner. This is known as the Pin 1 position. The socket has a matching marking.

Match the Pin 1 positions and place the processor carefully in the socket. Be extremely careful not to angle or twist the processor: if you bend or break the socket pins, the motherboard will be a write-off. The processor should drop easily into place. When you are sure that the pins and holes have connected, press it gently home.

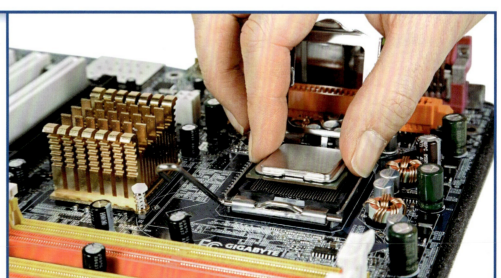

5 Lower the metal frame back onto the socket. It will cover the edge of the processor and hold it in place. Now lower the lever to 'lock' the socket.

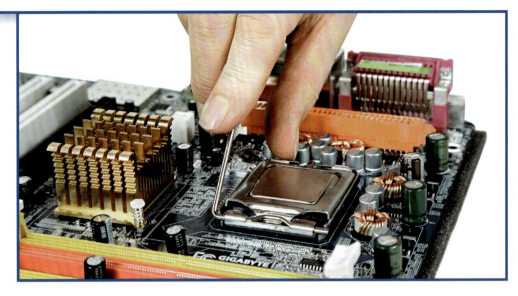

6 Clip the lever back into position alongside the socket. That's it – job done. The Pentium 4 processor has been successfully installed in the motherboard. However, were you to attempt to power the motherboard as things stand, the processor would overheat in a matter of seconds.

7 This is the cooling unit supplied with the processor, consisting of a heatsink with an integrated fan. As we remarked on p.42, it is always safer to buy a boxed processor that comes with a cooling unit than an 'OEM' package that comes without. Note the pad of grey goo on the base. This is thermal interface material used to ensure a good bond between the heatsink and the processor. Don't touch it. If your cooling unit has no such pre-applied material, see Steps 6 and 7 on p.114.

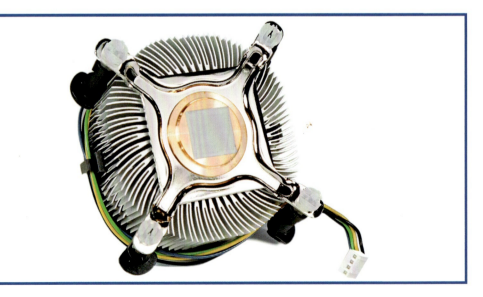

8

The cooling unit has four legs with a plastic push-pin on each. The motherboard has four matching holes for these pins positioned around the processor socket. Align the corners of the cooling unit with these holes.

9

Press down on the push-pins to lock them to the motherboard. Nothing will happen. Try again, but this time push harder. The degree of force required is truly disconcerting but it's absolutely essential to push the plastic pins firmly until they snap into the holes.

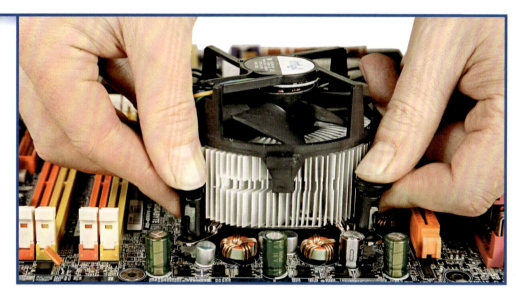

10

Finally, connect the cooling unit's power cable to the appropriate motherboard socket. This cable powers the fan whenever the computer is turned on. The socket should be stamped CPU FAN or similar and will certainly be located near the processor, but consult your motherboard manual if in any doubt. Ensure that the cable won't snag on the fan or any other motherboard components.

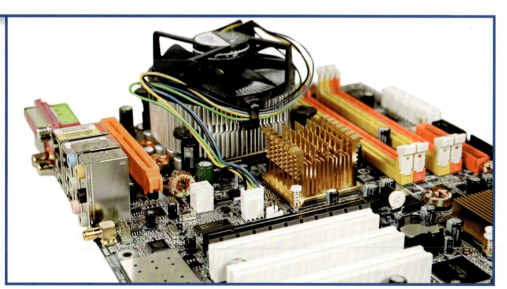

PART 3

Installing RAM

One other job that can be accomplished now while the motherboard remains conveniently outside the case is installing your memory modules.

As a rule, you should fill memory slots in the correct order. For instance, if your motherboard has four DIMMs, they will be numbered DIMM 1, DIMM 2 and so forth. If you have three memory modules, install the first in DIMM 1, followed by DIMM 2 and then DIMM 3. Don't leave gaps. Also check your motherboard manual carefully for specific requirements governing the use of single-sided or double-sided modules.

If your motherboard supports dual-channel memory, you have to take special care to install identical modules – same speed, same capacity, ideally from the same manufacturer – in matching pairs and in the right DIMMs. In the following example, the DIMMs are arranged in two pairs, each pair representing a channel. That is, DIMM 1 and DIMM 2 together are Channel A, and DIMM 3 and DIMM 4 are Channel B. For dual-channel operation, you must install one module in DIMM 1 (Channel A) and a matching module in DIMM 3 (Channel B). Slots are often colour-coded, which helps, but don't dive in until you're sure you know what goes where.

1

DIMM slots should be numbered on the motherboard but can otherwise be identified with the help of a schematic diagram in the motherboard manual. At either end of each slot are plastic retention clips. Flip these open on DIMM 1 by pushing them away from the slot. Now remove your first memory module from its antistatic bag. Hold it only by the ends to avoid contact with the memory chips or the lower connecting edge. Align the module carefully with the DIMM slot. The module and slot are both keyed with notches to ensure the correct orientation.

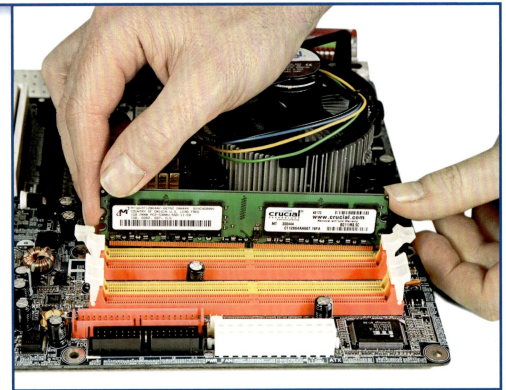

Push down on the module with your thumbs until the plastic clips snap shut. Again, you may be surprised or nervous about how much pressure you have to apply to coax the module into its new home. But take it easy, ensure that you keep the module vertical, and double-check that it is correctly aligned with the slot. Help the clips to close manually if you like.

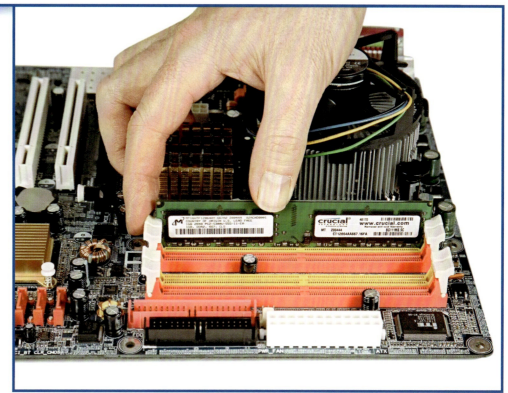

Now install the second module in the appropriate slot for dual-channel operation. Here, that means DIMM 3, which is colour-coded yellow to match DIMM 1. We now have a pair of matching modules ready to run at double the effective bandwidth.

PART 3 Installing the motherboard

Your motherboard is now host to a processor, a cooling unit and some memory. Unfortunately, that's about as far as we can go with the motherboard perched so conveniently on our antistatic mat. Now we need to install it in the case.

If your computer case has a removable tray, you should attach the motherboard to it before installing any other components. The advantage of the tray mechanism is that you don't have to fiddle with screws and standoffs inside the case.

Which is precisely what we'll do now with our tray-less case. Always work with the case on its side, so the motherboard goes in flat, and exercise caution: you wouldn't be the first to behead a capacitor with a slippery screwdriver. If your case has a power supply pre-installed, you may find that it partially blocks access to the motherboard. In this case, reverse Step 1 on p.95 to temporarily remove it in the meantime.

QUICK Q&A

My motherboard doesn't fit!
Actually, it does — unless, of course, you have made the mistake of obtaining an incompatible form factor. Industry standards guarantee that any ATX motherboard will fit any ATX case. However, this is not quite the same as saying that it will fit without a fiddle. You may find that the first couple of screws go in just fine but then the other holes appear to be slightly out of alignment. Motherboards are not inherently flexible but we have yet to be beaten by one, even when it took a measure of pushing and pulling and even a second pair of helping hands.

A removable tray makes it very much easier to fit the motherboard. The tray is then screwed back into place inside the case with the motherboard, processor and memory all onboard.

1

Strip the covers off your case. Here, the side panels are attached with thumbscrews so it's easy to remove them. You may need to use a screwdriver, brute force or your imagination. Because the case has no motherboard tray, there's a large flat panel inside. We'll attach the motherboard to this shortly.

2

Our case has a PSU in place. Spend a moment or two identifying the various types of power cable, and do what you have to do to clear the motherboard mounting. In this example, a cable runs from the PSU to the case fan, partially blocking access to the motherboard area. We have to unplug the mid-cable adapter – and then hopefully remember to reconnect it later.

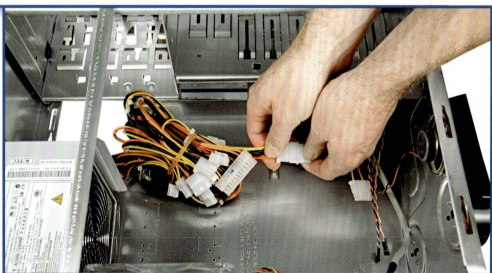

3

Your case will have an input/output shield fitted on the rear of the case. Unfortunately, this will almost certainly not match the inputs and outputs on your motherboard. However, your motherboard will have its own I/O shield in the box. Remove the original shield ...

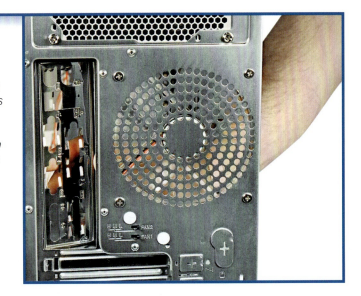

4

... and replace it with the new one. This is easier said than done, mind. I/O shields usually snap rather than screw into place. It can take considerable force to remove or fit a shield and they are wont to bend if you go overboard. Sharp edges lead all too easily to lacerated fingers. Take care.

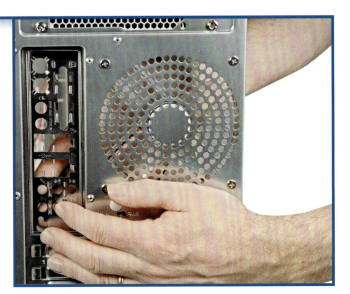

5

A motherboard is typically installed by screwing it to raised brass or plastic standoffs that must first be attached to the case or tray. You will find many more fittings for the standoffs than you actually need because the case will have been designed to accept a variety of motherboard sizes, including scaled-down ATX form factors. To determine where your standoffs should go, either hold the motherboard in place or follow the ATX markings in the case, if any.

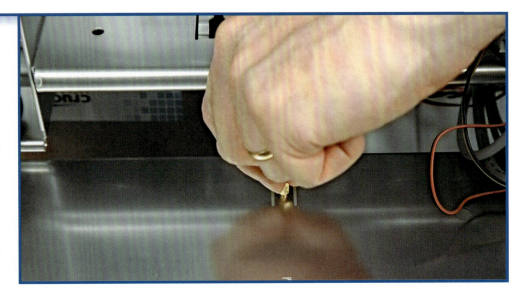

Holding the motherboard only by its edges, position it carefully inside the case. Check that there is a standoff in place for each hole in the motherboard. Don't be tempted to skip one and think it doesn't matter: we assure you that it does.

Align the motherboard's inputs and outputs with the I/O shield you fitted earlier. When the motherboard is correctly positioned on the screw standoffs, everything should match perfectly.

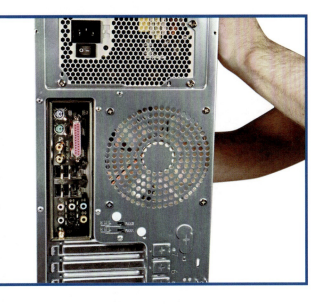

Finally, use the screws provided with the case to attach it to the standoffs. DO NOT over-tighten the screws as that risks cracking the motherboard. Should you drop a screw (you will, we promise), retrieve it with your trusty plastic pliers. Also take great care with your screwdriver – one slip-up here and you could easily trash the motherboard.

PART ③ Installing the PSU

If your case came with a PSU pre-installed, well and good. Often, though, the PSU will be a separate acquisition; and sometimes, especially in smaller cases, the PSU blocks access to the motherboard and must be temporarily removed before you can install the motherboard.

A smaller case has many advantages but working room is not one of them. Here, the PSU would have to come out if you wanted to work on – or install – the motherboard.

1

PSUs usually attach by means of four screws. The screw holes are positioned in such a way that the unit can only be installed in one orientation. It's a heavy beast, as you will now discover, so you may find a supporting shelf or ledge inside the case. Hold the PSU in position and screw it into place. Do not over-tighten the screws but ensure that the PSU has no room for movement.

2

Check that the PSU's power cables are all free-flowing, with nothing snagged or hidden. The first connection to make is the thick main power cable with its 24-pin plug (or 20-pin plug if you have an older motherboard). This connects to the main power socket on the motherboard, seen towards the top-right of this picture. It is keyed so it only fits one way round. If you're using an older motherboard with an early Pentium 4, look for the ATX 12V connection, too (see p.54).

③

Now connect the case fan or fans to the appropriate motherboard sockets. Each fan will likely have its own thin cable with a three-pin plug. Your motherboard manual will come in handy here for identifying the correct power sockets. Sometimes, however, fans use a cable adapter to connect to the PSU directly through a drive power cable rather than to the motherboard. In fact, we saw this arrangement in Step 2 on p.91.

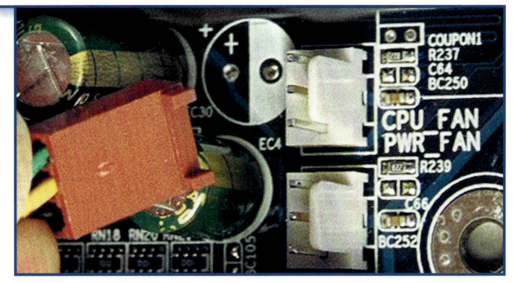

④

On behalf of the computer industry, please accept our heartfelt apologies at this juncture. It is time to wire-up a bunch of cables with tiny connectors that control various features on the front of the case, including the on/off and reset switches, the case lights and the speaker. Locate the relevant cluster of front panel sockets on the motherboard – it's at the top-right corner here – and take a deep breath. The tiny plugs may be named Speaker, Reset Switch and so forth – or they may not. The sockets may also be labelled – but not necessarily in the same way. The cables may even be colour-coded – but there's no guarantee that the motherboard will use the same colour-scheme.

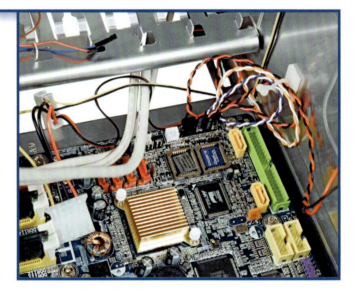

⑤

Additionally, none of these mini-plugs is keyed so it's all too easy to get the positive/negative polarity mixed up. All you can do is use whatever information the case and motherboard manuals provide between them. Later, if the LED lights on the front of the case fail to function when you power-up the PC, dive back in here and turn the 2-pin plugs through 180 degrees to reverse the polarity (see Techie Corner on p.97). The good news is that the power and reset switches will work regardless of polarity, but you must still connect the correct cables to the correct sockets to get the switches working.

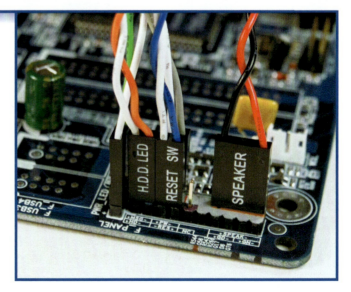

One final complication which you may or may not encounter. Our AOpen computer case is a fine and lovely thing, beautifully designed and easy to work with. Except for this. What you see here is the front port adapter intended to provide handy audio, USB and FireWire ports on the front of the case. However, these ports only work if you connect the adapter to the motherboard. The wired plugs were no problem but try as we might we simply could not figure out how to connect the snakes-nest of single cables correctly. In the end, we whipped the adapter out of the case and vowed to live without it.

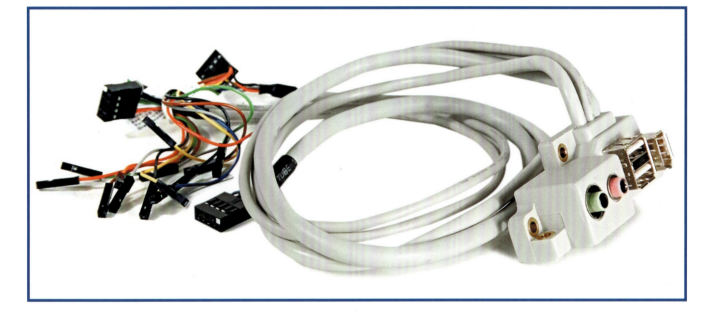

TECHIE CORNER

There is some merit in powering up the computer for the first time once you have made all the PSU connections. Without a keyboard, video card, monitor or hard disk, you're not going to get very far but you can at least check that the heatsink and case fans are working. You should also see a small light illuminate on the motherboard, which confirms that power is coming through.

Check that the PSU is set to the correct voltage – 220/230V in the UK – and connect it to the mains electricity with a female 3-pin power cable. Now turn the PSU's power switch to the On position and press the On/Off button on the front of the case. You needn't put the case covers on or even sit the case upright at this stage; this is a very simple test that won't take a moment. As the motherboard powers up, it should emit a series of coded beeps. You can interpret these codes if you have a mind to (p.158) but any beep at all is a sure sign of life. It also confirms that the case speaker is working. If you hear nothing, check the speaker cable connection. You also have an opportunity here to have a second bash at the front panel connections if you find that the lights or internal case speaker don't work. Switch off the power and unplug the power cable before making any internal adjustments!

When you're finished, turn off the computer with the case button, then switch the PSU to Off and unplug the power cable.

QUICK Q&A

This front panel business is too fiddly for words. Can't I connect these cables before the motherboard goes into the case?
Possibly. If your case has a removable motherboard tray, you may find that you can make the front panel cable connections before screwing the tray into the case. If your motherboard attaches directly to the case chassis, however, it is unlikely that the cables will stretch beyond the confines of the case to the motherboard lying on your mat. It's worth a try, though.

PART **3** # Installing the floppy disk drive

We will now install the first drive. As noted earlier, the floppy disk drive is rapidly approaching extinction, but we still have a soft spot for the old stalwart, especially when, as here, it is augmented with a memory card reader. See also p.132 for a word on why you may just need a floppy drive.

1

The precise procedure for installing any drive depends upon the specific design of your case. Here, we must first remove the front fascia to gain access to the drive bays. The fascia has drive bay covers which pop off with a good prod. But not yet ...

2

Thus exposed, we can see the drive bays inside the case. There are secondary internal drive bay covers here covering all but two bays: one each in the upper 5.25-inch section and the lower 3.5-inch drive area. Remove the corresponding drive bay covers from the fascia. If you're going to install two optical drives, also remove the internal and external covers from a second drive bay.

Before installing the drive, familiarise yourself with its cable connections. A standard floppy (left) requires a 'Berg' power cable and a ribbon cable connection to the motherboard; but our memory card reader (right) also has a USB cable. Note the twist in the ribbon cable. This end always goes to the drive, not to the motherboard. The cable also has a red or pink edge which must be matched to Pin 1 position on the drive.

Replace the fascia and slide the drive into the drive bay from the outside in. Ensure that the front of the drive is flush with the front of the case; or, if your case has a curved or shaped fascia, is set neither too far back to be accessible nor too far forward.

5

The drive must be secured internally. This usually means screwing it into place with two screws on either side, as shown in this picture. However, our case uses an innovative self-locking system that makes for easy installation and removal. We'll see it in action when we install the DVD drive.

Connect the ribbon cable to the rear of the drive and plug in a Berg-style power cable from the PSU.

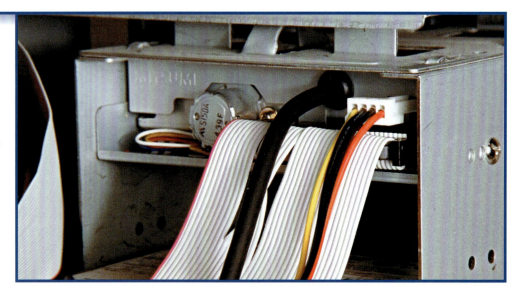

6

Connect the other end of the ribbon cable to the floppy drive controller socket on the motherboard. Consult the manual for directions if necessary. The plug and socket may or may not be keyed to prevent erroneous installation: if not, look for a Pin 1 marking on the socket (or in the manual) and match this to the striped edge of the cable. Push home firmly.

7

Finally, connect the USB cable (if present) to a USB socket on the motherboard (again, if present). Most motherboards provide a pair of internal USB sockets for purposes just like this. *See p.120 for one that does not.*

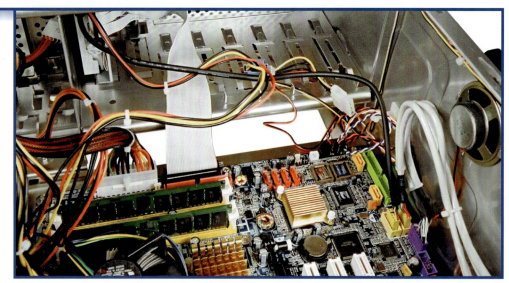

PART 3 Installing the DVD drive

Optical drives – CD and DVD in all their fancy flavours – use 5.25-inch drive bays. Our case has four such bays but yours may have one, two, three or more, depending on its height. We will install a single DVD writer drive.

Before you begin, prepare your drive. If you have an ATA-style drive, you'll find a jumper panel around the back. The position of the shunt on an array of pins determines whether this drive is the master or slave device on the IDE/ATA channel. Two drives can share a channel (and hence a motherboard socket) but only if the jumpers are correctly set so that one is the master and one the slave. Make your first or only drive the master.

Alternatively, and better, set the jumpers to the Cable Select position and use an 80-conductor cable. If you later install a second drive on the same channel, set it to Cable Select too. You'll need your pointy pliers for jumper work (or long nails). Better still, buy a drive with a SATA interface.

Most modern drives have two audio outputs – 4-pin analogue and 2-pin digital – and most sound cards or motherboards with integrated audio have corresponding sockets of both types. However, thanks to a process known as Digital Audio Extraction, it is almost always possible to dispense with audio cables altogether. If a drive supports DAE – and any new drive will for sure – then the sound signal is channelled to the sound card through the IDE/ATA bus instead.

? QUICK Q&A

Does it matter which drive I make the master and which the slave?
No. All that matters from your computer's point of view is that it can tell one channel-sharing drive from the other. The master/slave nomenclature is misleading because neither drive has priority over the other. If you only install one drive on a channel, you should of course make it the master device.

Here we have a drive all wired up and ready to go, with an audio cable to the left and a ribbon cable to the right. Note that this is a 40-conductor cable so the jumpers have been set to the master position rather than to Cable Select. Note too that the striped edge of the cable matches Pin 1 position on the drive.

👓 TECHIE CORNER

Anatomy of an IDE/ATA cable A standard 80-conductor has three plugs. One end, often coloured blue, connects to the motherboard socket. At the opposite end is the master device plug, usually coloured black. Whichever drive you plug this into is automatically assigned master status on the ITE/ATA channel so long as the drive's jumpers are set to the Cable Select position. The slave device plug, usually coloured grey, is located about a third of the way along the cable from the master plug.
Older 40-conductor cables cannot determine the status of a device so it doesn't matter which plug you connect to which drive. The master/slave business must be controlled entirely by the drive jumpers.

An 80-conductor IDE/ATA cable has 80 fine wires, three coloured plugs, a red Pin 1 stripe and a built-in brain of sorts.

①

If you haven't already done so, snap/poke/pull/push off a 5.25-inch drive bay cover. Now slide the drive into the bay, align it with the front of the fascia, screw it into place and connect the ribbon and power (Molex) cables. Connect the other end of the ribbon cable to the secondary IDE/ATA socket on the motherboard, leaving the primary IDE/ATA channel free for the hard drive.

Unless, that is, you are going to install a SATA hard drive, as we are, in which case you can use the primary (or sole) IDE/ATA channel. Again, match Pin 1 on the socket with the stripe on the cable.

②

If you install two optical drives in your computer, or plan to in the future, install the first in the uppermost drive bay. The layout of the connectors on the ribbon cable makes it easier to install an additional channel-sharing drive when the second drive is located below the first.

③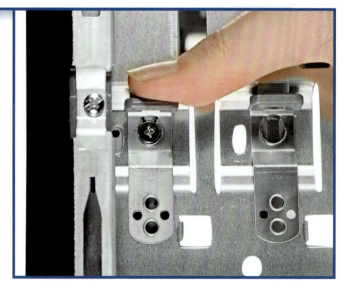

Our case uses an ingenious drive-fastening mechanism that repays a quick look. It works on the principle of spring-loaded clasps, the benefit being that you can remove a drive in the future without having to unscrew it.

④

You do, however, need a screwdriver to begin with. Affix one screw to each side of the drive but don't tighten them fully. Special screws are provided for this.

④

Now slide the drive into the drive bay. The spring-loaded mechanism catches the screws and locks the drive into place. It's much easier than fiddling with a screwdriver inside the case and you can release the drive at any time simply by releasing the catch.

❻

From the outside, our project is beginning to look like a proper computer. You could at this point add an extra optical drive or two but we recommend that you get your PC up and running in a fairly minimal configuration first. Any problems – not that you should have any – are easier to diagnose and fix this way.

PART 3 Installing the hard disks

Installing a hard disk drive is very similar to installing an optical drive, including the same jumper and master/slave considerations. However, our project PC uses the newer and simpler SATA interface. We're going to install a pair. See p.142 for the reason why.

See p.142 for the reason why.

? QUICK Q&A

How do I work out where the jumpers are supposed to be on my IDE/ATA drive?
The hard disk drive case should have a printed diagram that illustrates all the possible jumper configurations. In our experience, however, some don't. If the drive was supplied with a manual or even a scrap of paper, look to it for instructions; if not, check the manufacturer's website. A company called Ontrack also maintains a very useful online database of drive/jumper details. See Appendix 4 for contact details.

Remember to set the jumpers before you install your drive. If two drives are going to share an IDE/ATA channel, one must be made the master and one the slave. Or, again, use Cable Select and an 80-conductor cable. You should not install hard drives and optical drives on the same channel.

SATA does away with ribbon cables in favour of a thinner, more malleable data cable (the blue cable in this picture). The power cable also has a new plug so be sure you have a SATA-enabled PSU or a cable adapter.

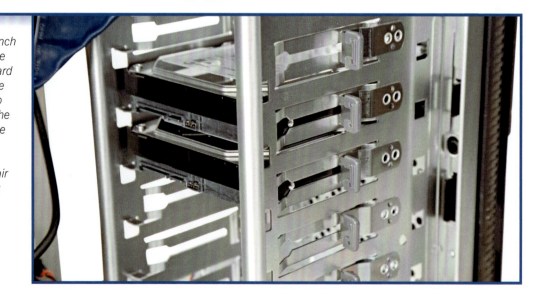

1

Slide your drive into a 3.5-inch internal drive bay. Unlike the floppy and DVD drives, a hard drive needs no access to the outside world and so has no corresponding opening on the case fascia. Screw into place or, as here, use the drive retention provided by your case. We've installed our pair next to one another but you could leave a space.

If you are installing an IDE/ATA drive, connect the ribbon cable to drive and to the IDE/ATA socket on the motherboard. As ever, match Pin 1.

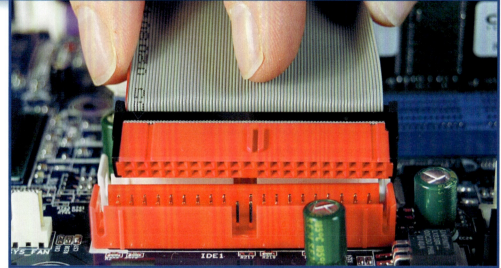

With SATA drives, each device connects to its own motherboard socket so there is no channel sharing to worry about. Check your motherboard for instructions as to which of the SATA sockets to use. It may not matter, but it might. If you remember, ours provides eight SATA I sockets and 2 SATA II sockets.

4

Connect the power cable, be it Molex or SATA. In both cases, the plugs and sockets are shaped to ensure that it is impossible to connect the cable incorrectly.

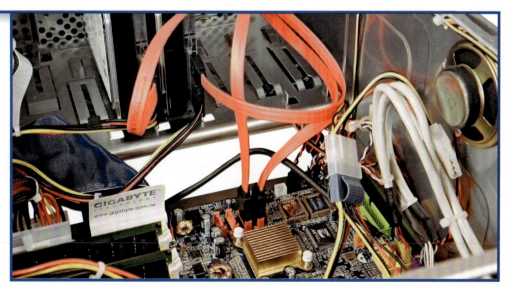

PART ③ Installing the video card

Our PC is coming along very nicely. The motherboard is installed in the case, the processor, heatsink and memory modules are all attached and we've connected a floppy disk drive, a couple of hard disks, and a DVD drive. Next we will install a video card.

The procedure for installing any expansion card is basically the same. However, 4x-speed and faster AGP video cards and the latest PCI Express 16x-speed cards have a 'tail' that must be secured in the slot. This is simply because they usually carry weighty cooling systems and without an extra retention mechanism they would be unstable in the slot.

❶

Locate the AGP or PCI Express 16x-speed slot on your motherboard and remove the corresponding blanking plate from the case. It may need unscrewing, in which case keep the screw, or it may slide or pop out.

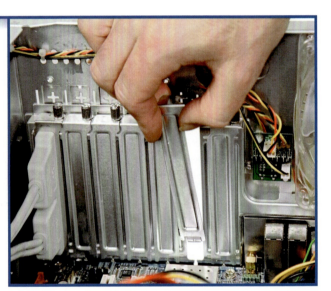

Plain PCI cards are light enough to stand upright in a slot once installed but AGP and PCI Express video cards need a helping hand, or tail.

Remove the video card from its protective antistatic packaging. You should still be wearing your antistatic wrist-strap and using an antistatic mat, of course. Be careful not to touch the electrical contacts on the bottom edge – greasy fingerprints are lousy for connectivity – or any of the onboard components. Position the card in the AGP or PCI Express slot, releasing and then securing the card retention mechanism (usually a spring-loaded plastic pin). Push down on the card quite firmly until it's securely seated in the slot. This is an AGP card ...

... and this is a PCI Express card in situ. The difference from the perspective of installation is virtually nil, other than using a different slot.

Screw, clip or otherwise attach the port end of the card to the case chassis. In our experience tiny variations in card size and case design mean you don't always get a perfect match between card and case, but with a little manoeuvring you should be able to secure the card in place. Make absolutely sure that the card is fully seated in the slot.

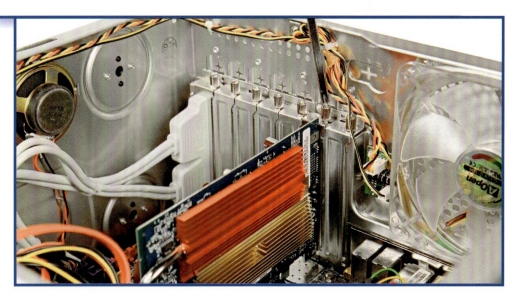

Not really a step, merely an observation. This AGP card comes perilously close to overhanging the neighbouring PCI slot (we'll see a similar issue on p.123). There is still some clearance but installing a card next to it would certainly impede airflow to the video card's fan. If you have a port bracket to install, this would be the best PCI slot to sacrifice (see p.139).

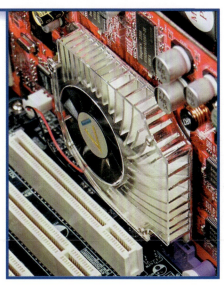

TECHIE CORNER

If you have procured a motherboard with onboard video, you will need to connect the supplied VGA port bracket to the video chip on the motherboard. The bracket will have a cable and plug pre-fitted so consult the manual and find the right socket on the motherboard. Then remove a blanking plate, as in Step 1, and screw the bracket into place. This simple procedure gives your computer an external VGA port to which a monitor may be attached.

Should you later wish to upgrade to a standalone video card, you might have to manually disable the onboard video chip. We say 'might' because some motherboards automatically disable integrated video in favour of an AGP or PCI Express card as soon as one is installed. This is a query for your motherboard manual.

4

PART 4 Assembling an Athlon SFF PC

In the previous project, we could just as easily have used an AMD processor and virtually everything would have been identical save for a slightly altered processor and heatsink installation. But now it's time to build an altogether different PC. This time we will base it around an Athlon 64 FX chip.

PART 4 Upfront preparation

In the previous project, the motherboard and case came separately. But with a 'barebones' small form factor (SFF) kit such as the Shuttle SN95G5, the computer is already half-built. The motherboard and PSU are both pre-installed, so there's no need to fit standoffs or fiddle with the rear input/output panel and those awkward front panel connections. This makes assembly very much quicker. The only real downside is that your working space is much reduced.

Your first task with any barebones kit is to disassemble it. It's well worth making notes as you go along here or even snapping your own step-by-step photos with a digital camera, for it all has to go back together in exactly the same way. The exact routine obviously varies according to the model but the goal is the same: an empty box with just the motherboard and PSU remaining. Please note that you should leave the main PSU power cable connected to the motherboard throughout; or, if you find that it is not connected when you strip the case, plug it in at the outset.

1

The SN95G5 is a fairly typical cube-shaped SFF PC. This is what it looks like straight out of the box and also what it will look like when it's finished. But right now, our barebones kit has nothing much inside. Unscrew the thumbscrews on the rear to get inside.

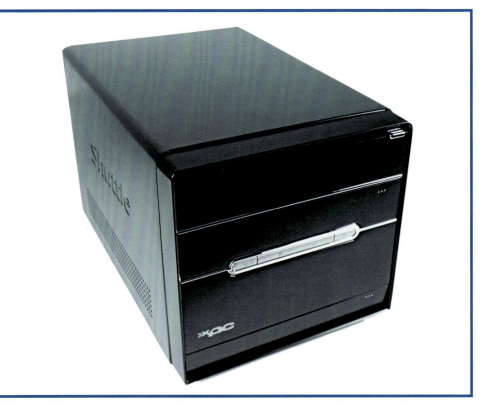

2

Slide the single cover towards the rear and upwards to free it. Now lift it off completely and put it somewhere safe. If we mentioned that we once managed to sit on a flimsy SFF case cover, you'd only laugh – but it was no fun at the time.

3

With space at such a premium inside this box, everything fits together very precisely indeed and there's not a wasted square centimetre. In fact, there's no way to access the motherboard unless you first remove the drive bay cage. This unscrews and lifts out completely.

4

You must also remove the cooling system. This is a proprietary design, seen here in isolation. The fan is attached to the vent on the rear of the case and connected to the heatsink by means of cooling pipes. The bracket is used to secure the heatsink to the processor socket. Note the power cable and remember to plug this into the motherboard later.

PART ④ Fleshing out the barebones

We can't work with the motherboard outside the case here as we did on p.84–89 so be prepared for some nimble finger work. If you were installing an Athlon processor in a 'normal' tower-style PC, you would probably use the cooling system supplied with the processor. In that case, the installation procedure would be very similar indeed to the Pentium 4 routine. Here, there's simply no room for a standard heatsink or fan so it all gets a bit more complicated. But only a bit.

❶

We can see the Socket 939 design for Athlon 64 and 64 FX on the Shuttle motherboard. It's basically similar to the Pentium 4 Socket 775 with one key difference: here, the socket has holes and the processor has the pins.

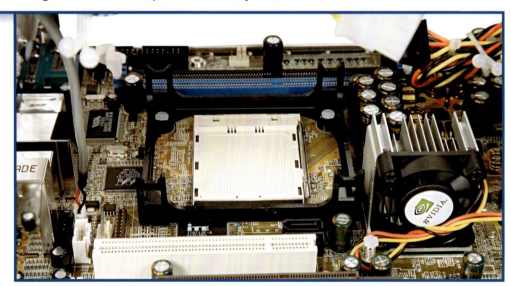

❷

Lift the lever that runs adjacent to the socket to its fully upright position. This opens the pin holes and prepares the socket to receive the processor.

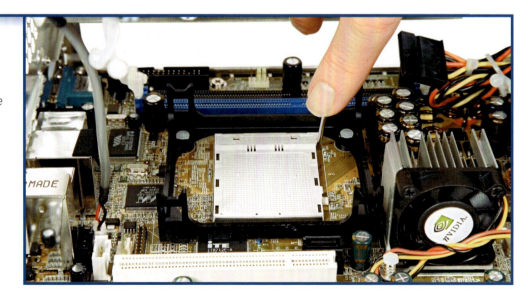

Handle your Athlon processor with great care. If you bend a pin, the damage is permanent. Look for the gold triangle in one corner (top-left here). This denotes the Pin 1 position. You must match this triangle to a similar marking on the processor slot.

Carefully lower the processor onto the socket, checking that the lever is still upright and that you have matched Pin 1 positions. The processor can only be installed in one orientation and the pins and pin holes should match perfectly.

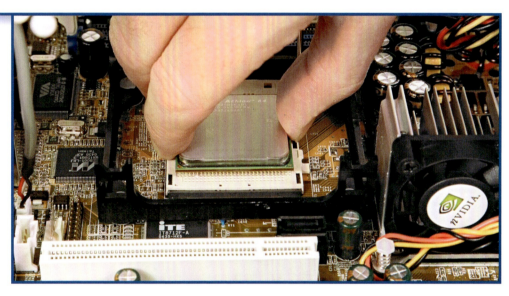

Gently press the processor home in the socket. It should lie completely flat and flush. If you have the slightest doubt, double-check that you are matching Pin 1 on the processor with Pin 1 on the socket. You can see the gold triangle marking on the upper side of the processor as well as on the pin side.

Back on p.86, our Pentium 4 cooling unit came with a pre-applied thermal interface, but our Shuttle cooling unit does not. Instead, it is supplied with a sachet of thermal glue. Squeeze the full amount onto the centre of the processor.

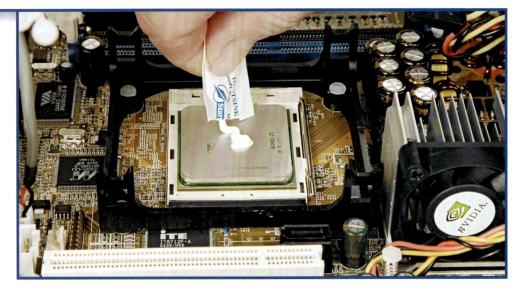

Spread it out more or less evenly over the square, silver part of the processor using a business card or something similar. The purpose of this glue is not to stick the cooling unit in place but rather to ensure the best possible conductive bond. Without it, the cooling unit would not be able to draw away sufficient heat from the processor.

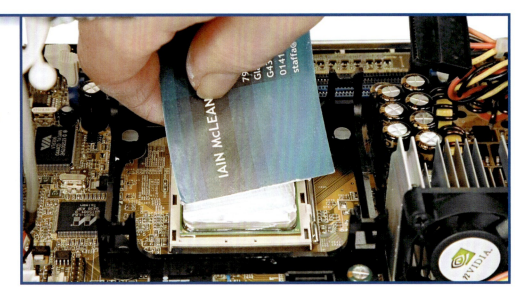

Now for the tricky part. Lower the cooling unit onto the frame that surrounds the processor socket. The unit is attached to a fan with pipes and the fan goes to the rear of the case, so there's no room for doubt over which way it goes. However, try to get it right first time to avoid spreading the thermal gunk all over the place.

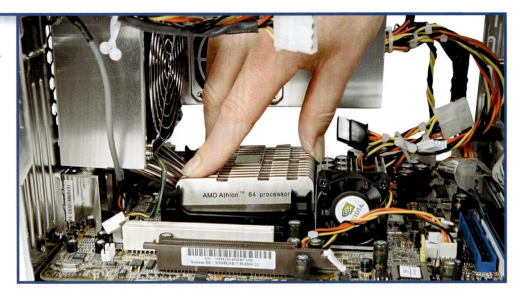

9

Press the heatsink firmly into the socket frame and onto the processor. Now place the retention frame over the heatsink. One side has an obvious tab, which we'll need in the next step. Meanwhile, hook the catches on the opposite sides into the holes in the raised arms of the socket frame.

10

Carefully, but with a measure of brute force, press down on the retention frame tab to hook the remaining two catches into the retention frame's arms. You may need a few goes at this – we did, anyway – but that's okay so long as you don't overly disturb the heatsink.

11

Plug the cooling unit's power cable into the appropriate socket on the motherboard. In this example, it is clearly labelled and located conveniently close to the socket.

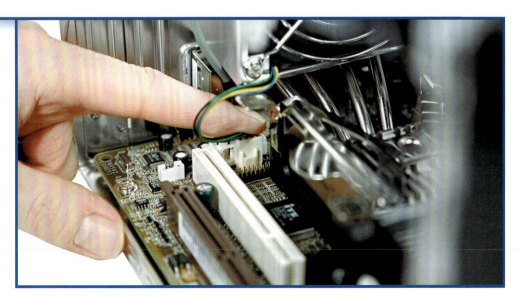

12

Now secure the fan section of the cooling unit to the grille on the rear of the case, using the four thumbscrews provided.

13

Looking down on the finished installation with the integrated power cables pulled out of the way, we can see the retention frame in place over the heatsink and the fan attached to the rear of the case (to the right here). That's the hard part over.

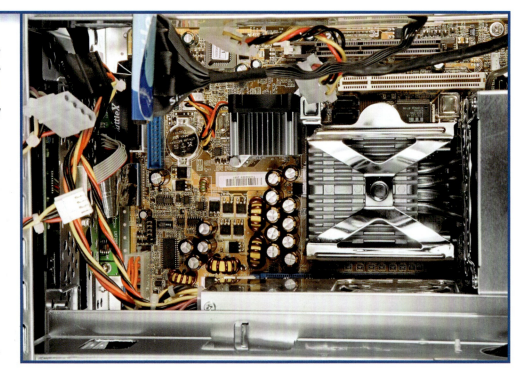

14

Let's move straight onto the memory installation. Just as on p.88–89, open the catches at either end of the first DIMM slot and carefully align your first memory module. Hold it vertical and match the notches on its lower edge with the notches in the slot. If you are installing a single module, use DIMM 1.

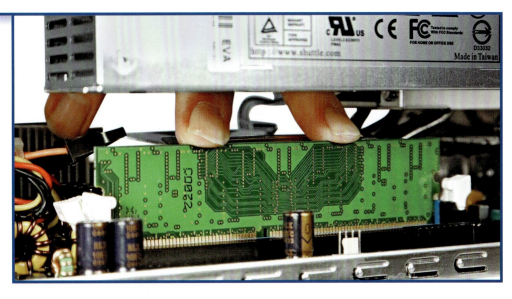

15

Press down firmly on the module to snap the slot catches shut. The module must be completely level in the slot. Again, it's all a bit cramped in here so take care.

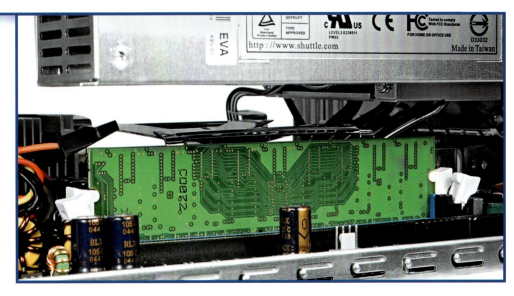

16

This Shuttle motherboard supports dual-channel memory (DDR only, not DDR2) so we'll install a second, identical module in DIMM 2. That's all that's required to double the memory bandwidth, for the chipset takes care of everything else automatically.

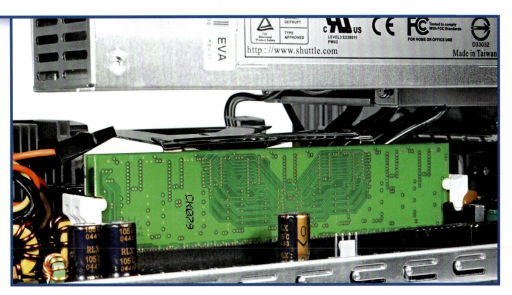

PART ④ Installing the drives

Our SFF kit has room for one hard disk drive, one floppy drive (or, optionally, a second hard disk) and one optical drive. The installation procedure is quite different from that of a tower case but clever design makes it straightforward. Here we'll install three drives in one easy procedure.

❶

In Step 3 on p.111, we removed the drive bay cage. The hard drive can now be screwed into this cage in the standard manner i.e. with four screws. Check how the cage fits within the case and be sure to install the drive so that its rear end – the end with the sockets – faces into the case.

❷

Now is the time to think about jumper configurations if you're using an IDE/ATA drive. Ours is SATA so these concerns don't apply. Slide the drive bay cage into the case with the drive in situ and reattach it with the screws you removed earlier.

3

You'll find that the power cable is routed around the side of the case from the PSU to just the right position. Connect this to the hard drive. Here it's a SATA-style power cable. Then connect the supplied data cable – again, we're dealing with SATA – to the drive.

4

Plug the other end of the data cable into the motherboard socket. Our motherboard has SATA and IDE/ATA sockets but we're only interested in the first SATA channel. The hard drive is now ready to run.

⑤

There's space above the hard disk drive for a floppy drive or a second hard disk drive. We'll plump for the same floppy/memory card reader drive you saw earlier. Slide the drive into place in the cage. It is possible to attach it to the cage at the same time as the hard drive (see Step 1), i.e. while the cage is outside the case. However, it's important to align the front of the drive with the drive opening on the case fascia and this is easier when the cage has already been installed.

⑥

When correctly aligned so that the front of the drive is flush with the fascia, screw the drive in place in the cage. Now connect the supplied (short) floppy drive cable to both drive and motherboard socket. Also connect the PSU power cable to the drive.

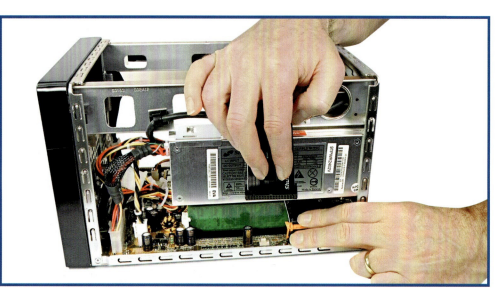

⑦

As this drive requires an internal USB connection to control the memory card reader, connect the drive's USB cable to a USB socket on the motherboard. Er, except that we discovered that we couldn't. This motherboard has two USB sockets but they are the wrong shape for our drive's plug. The result was that we couldn't use the drive as a memory card reader. If there's a lesson to be learned here, it's the one we set out on p.77: buy your motherboard (or barebones kit) first and study it before buying other components. Compatibility simply can't be taken for granted.

*Slide your optical drive into the
vacant 5.25-inch section of
the drive bay cage but don't
screw it in place just yet.*

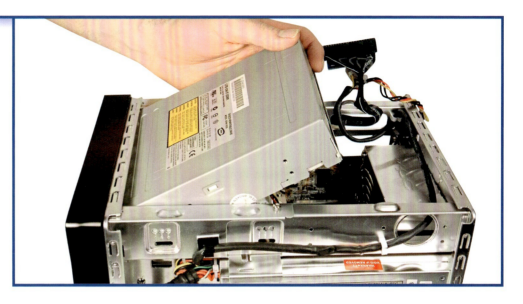

*This case design keeps the
optical drive hidden behind a
panel. To access the drive, you
press a small button on the
front of the case. This is not
an electrical operation but
rather a mechanical lever that
activates the tray-opening
button on the drive. You may
need to adjust the mechanism
slightly in order to align the
pressure pad on the lever with
the drive's button. This sounds
more complicated than it is.*

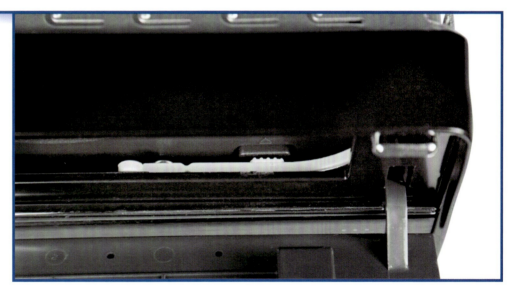

*Connect the power and data
cables to the drive and the
data cable to the
motherboard. Again, a special
short data cable is provided. If
you were using a SATA drive,
you would use the second
SATA motherboard channel.
Finally, screw the optical drive
to the drive cage.*

PART 4 Installing the video and expansion cards

This barebones kit has two slots: a fast AGP 8x-speed slot for a video card and a plain old-fashioned PCI card for anything else you fancy. But only one of anything you fancy, mind. We'll install a Wi-Fi card but you may prefer a TV tuner card, particularly if you want to run Windows Media Center or similar on your PC.

This Shuttle case has a catch mechanism for securing expansion cards. Lift this and remove the two blanking plates. Now install the PCI card in the PCI slot. Our Wi-Fi card has an aerial on its faceplate so extra care is required.

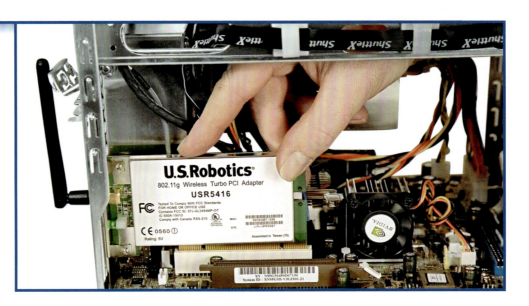

Install the video card next. Because this is a high-speed AGP card, it has a tail that must be secured in the slot with a retention clip. Note that we have customised this card by removing its original cooling unit and fitting a silent fan-free heatsink in its place. See Step 4 for more on this.

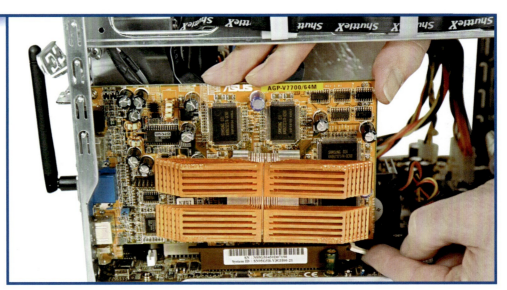

3

Close the expansion card catch and screw it in place. This secures the two cards in place.

4

As you can see from this angle, the video card's silent heatsink comes perilously close to the edge of the case and looks like it will only just clear the cover. The fact is that some cards have such bulky cooling units that they simply don't fit. For instance, the video card we used in the Pentium 4 tower project earlier would be far too wide for this SFF case. It's well worth checking the support and user forum sections of the case or kit manufacturer's website for guidance as problematic cards may be known and flagged as such.

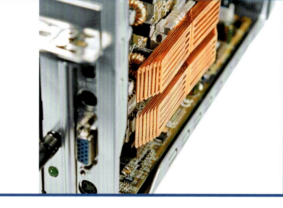

5

Make a final check of the internal connections, checking that the main power cable is still connected to the motherboard. Now, with the case cover back on and secured with thumbscrews, and with a power cable connected, our mini PC is effectively ready to go.

6

But first, just check that the optical drive release mechanism works (see Step 9 on p.121). With the power on, the drive tray should open when you press the silver button in the top-right corner. If the masking panel fails to flip open like this, adjust the release mechanism until it does.

5

PART **5** **Final touches**

We told you it was easy. All that remains now is to set up the computer to behave to your liking, install an operating system and finish off with a final expansion card. We will cover trouble-shooting in some detail, too, just in case of problems.

PART ⑤ Connecting a monitor and switching on

At this point in the proceedings, you might be tempted to rush into further installations: the sound card, perhaps, or an internal modem or network card. However, now is the time to establish that everything has gone according to plan so far. Adding extra components merely complicates trouble-shooting, should any be required.

With a monitor and keyboard connected, and optionally a mouse, give your new computer its first trial run.

Check it out

Give your work-in-progress a thorough once-over. Check that the heatsink and case fans are all still connected to the motherboard, that the memory modules are still clipped into their DIMMs, that the drives are all wired-up with ribbon and power cables, and that the video card is fully secured in its slot. You might like to reassemble the case now but it's not strictly necessary. You can even leave the case lying on its side to better monitor the action. However … you will be working with live electricity from here on so never touch anything inside your PC's case while the PSU is connected to the mains power. Even when you turn off your computer, the PSU continues to draw power from the mains and the motherboard remains in a partially-powered standby state. We're only talking a 5V current, to be fair, but it's simply crazy to work on a 'live' motherboard or anything connected to it.

True, you could flip the PSU to Off (if it has its own power switch) and/or turn off the electricity at the wall socket (and hope that Junior doesn't turn it back on for a laugh while your head is buried in the case), but it's better and safer to get into the habit of always removing the power cable before conducting any internal work. This is the only cast-iron way to ensure no physical connection between yourself and the National Grid.

Booting up ... and down again

Connect the monitor to the video card's VGA or DVI port and plug it in to the mains. Also connect a PS/2-style keyboard (see the Techie Corner). Turn on the monitor now. You might see a 'no signal' or similar message on the screen.

Now check that the PSU is set to the correct voltage – 220/230V in the UK – and connect it to the mains with your second power cable. Flip the PSU's power switch to the on position. Finally, press the on/off button on the front of the case. Your PC will come to life for the first time.

Look inside the case and check – by observation, not by touch – that the heatsink and case fans are whirring. If not, kill the mains power immediately and check the fan cable connections on the motherboard. Ignore any beeps for now.

All being well, power your computer down with the on/off button and unplug the power cable. Leave the power switch on the PSU at the on position from now on. If all is not well, skip to p.148 now for some trouble-shooting procedures.

Let us now turn our attention to some important configuration settings.

Powering up our Pentium PC for the first time.

PART ⑤ BIOS setup

FINAL TOUCHES

When you're used to a working in a Windows environment,
the text-only world of BIOS menus can seem a little daunting.
You can certainly temporarily cripple your computer if you
make careless changes so do tread carefully.

CMOS and BIOS

CMOS (Complementary Metal-Oxide Semiconductor) is a special kind of small-scale memory embedded in a chip soldered to the motherboard and powered by a battery. It maintains a record of the date and time, how much memory your PC has and which hardware devices are attached. It is only by reference to CMOS during the power-up procedure that the computer knows it is a computer at all and not, for instance, a peach. Without CMOS, it would have to laboriously re-identify itself every time.

CMOS is not something that need concern you during the everyday operation of your computer but it does require some configuration at the outset. This is handled through the BIOS setup program.

BIOS ROM (Basic Input/Output System Read-Only Memory) is a separate chip on the motherboard that contains – or, rather, that is – a set of instructions and drivers intended to get the computer up and running before Windows (or any other operating system) kicks in. BIOS lets you manually configure the information held in CMOS. To access its Setup program, you

must press a specific key or combination of keys as the computer is powering up. Your motherboard manual should make this clear but the chances are that it's Delete, Escape, F1 or F2. You may see 'Press DEL to enter SETUP' or a similar message appear on screen as the computer starts. If you don't see any prompts and the manual draws a blank, repeatedly press the Delete, Escape, F1 or F2 keys as soon as the computer's POST procedure (p.151) completes its memory count.

Reconnect your power cable now, turn on your computer and find your way into the BIOS setup program.

BIOS basics

There are, inevitably, many BIOS programs around. In the following example, we will be working with the Award-made BIOS program used on our Gigabyte motherboard. You should be able to interpret your own motherboard's BIOS in a similar manner, even if it looks rather different.

Working with BIOS is a matter of selecting options on menus,

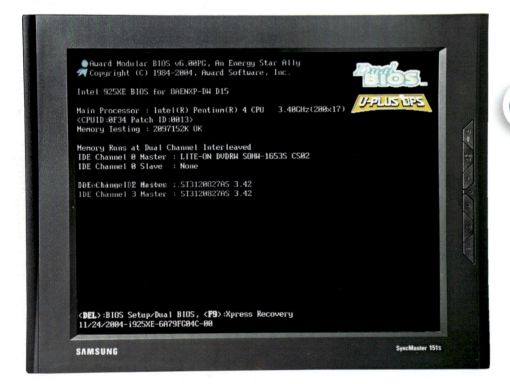

Watch the screen closely for clues about getting into BIOS. Here it is merely a matter of hitting the Delete key at the right time.

TECHIE CORNER

A modern Plug-and-Play BIOS will automatically detect and configure a hard disk drive. This is exceedingly useful as it saves you having to manually enter information about cylinders, heads, landing zones, sectors, access modes and the like. This information can be gleaned from the drive's manual, of course, or perhaps from a printed panel on the drive itself, or at least from the manufacturer's website if all else fails. But it's a definite hassle and it's all too easy to get a setting wrong. However, do see the following section for a cautionary word on SATA.

making changes where necessary and then saving these changes to CMOS. The BIOS setup program should include a guide as to which keyboard keys govern each action; if not, press F1 for help. These are the keys that control our Award BIOS:

Up Arrow	Move to previous item on a menu
Down Arrow	Move to the next item on a menu
Left Arrow	Move to an item to the left of the current position
Right Arrow	Move to an item to the right of the current position
Escape	Quit the current menu
Page Up	Increase the selected item's current numeric value
Page Down	Decrease the selected item's current numeric value
F1	BIOS help
Enter	Confirm a selection
F10	Exit BIOS and save changes

Tweaking BIOS

We are concerned with three settings here. We want to set the date and time, turn on the motherboard's onboard wireless networking (Wi-Fi), and enable the optical drive as a bootable device so that we can install Windows.

The computer's time and date settings are found within a CMOS sub-menu. Use the up/down/left/right arrow keys to select (highlight) a menu option called Standard CMOS Features – it's at the top of the left-hand column here – and press Enter to access the sub-menu.

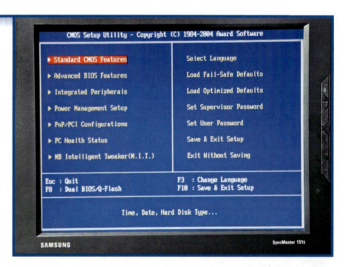

You may find that the date and time are already correct because the motherboard manufacturer pre-set them in the factory. If not, select each entry in turn with the arrow keys and then press Page Up or Page Down to change the value. For instance, if the month entry currently says January but it's really July, select Jan and press the Page Down key repeatedly until July appears. Now press Enter to confirm the change and move onto the next entry with the arrow keys. When you're finished, press Escape to return to the main menu page.

3

The wireless networking setting is tucked away within the Integrated Peripherals sub-menu. Select this now and press Enter to get to the sub-menu.

4

Move the selection to the Enabled field and press Enter. Wi-Fi should now be operational. You would now want to return to the previous screen and enable integrated audio (Azalia Codec), 1394 (FireWire), SATA support and, perhaps, USB keyboard and mouse support.

5

Next, highlight Advanced BIOS Features and press Enter. Here, we see the order in which the computer looks to its drives as it powers up. Select the first boot device entry, press Enter, and change the setting to CDROM. You will now be able to install Windows directly from the CD. Later, return here and reset the hard disk as the first bootable device.

When exiting the BIOS setup program, it is important to save your changes to CMOS. Return to the main menu by pressing Escape. Press Escape again and then, when prompted, confirm that you want to save your changes by pressing Y. Alternatively, press F10 at any time to save your changes and exit BIOS in one move. Should you ever make a mistake or lose your place, simply type N when exiting and the CMOS record will not be altered or updated. If you forget to save your changes, you can always go back and do it all again. We are only scratching the surface of BIOS here: see your motherboard manual for full details.

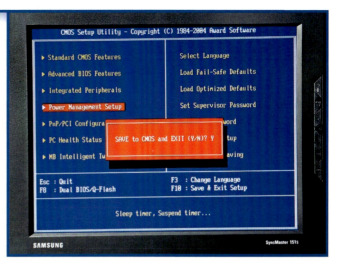

QUICK Q&A
What happens if the CMOS battery runs out?
This dilemma is more commonly posed as a hypothesis than encountered as a reality. CMOS runs on very little power indeed and its battery should last for years and years. A good clue that the battery is failing is continually having to reset the date and time. The proper action is, of course, to replace the battery while the computer is turned off. Before starting, make a hand-written record of all the screens in the BIOS setup program. You can then re-enter this information through BIOS when the new battery is installed.

Be sure to buy the right kind of battery for your motherboard: usually but not always 3V. It's also worth trying to install your new battery as quickly as you possibly can. The original CMOS record just might survive a second or two without power, in which case you can reboot and carry on exactly where you left off.

BIOS updates

Motherboard manufacturers buy BIOS programs from a select few suppliers, including Phoenix Technologies (which now includes Award) and AMI. From time to time, such as when considering a processor upgrade or trying to enable support for a new technology without throwing out the motherboard, you may find it beneficial or even essential to upgrade the BIOS. No soldering iron is required; all BIOS chips these days are 'flash' upgradeable, which means you can download and install an update from the manufacturer's website. You certainly won't need a new BIOS when starting off with a new, recently-made motherboard, however, and a non-essential BIOS update is not the best use of a slow Sunday afternoon (for which read: if it ain't broke, leave well alone).

Flash upgrade procedures vary but generally you download a couple of files from the internet, copy them to a floppy disk, enable the floppy disk drive as the first bootable device in your computer (back to BIOS again) and then run a setup program that automatically installs the new BIOS.

The most important thing is to remember to make a copy of the CMOS record before starting out, just in case the upgrade fails halfway through and wipes the current settings. To do this, run the BIOS setup program and copy down everything you see.

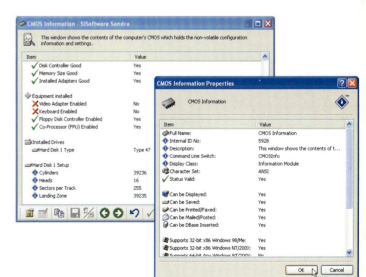

A software utility like SiSoft Sandra can help you glean vital information from CMOS (see Appendix 4).

PART ⑤ Installing Windows XP

With the CD drive enabled as a boot device, you can now install Windows straight from the installation CD without using floppies. We will describe the Windows XP Home Edition procedure here but XP Professional installs in an almost identical manner.

As you probably know, Windows XP must be 'activated' with Microsoft to keep it working beyond an initial 30-day grace period. Because this procedure is sensitive to system changes – e.g. a major upgrade or component replacement can make XP demand re-activation – we would suggest that you postpone activation until you are happy with your overall hardware configuration.

Sit your computer upright on the table, connect a mouse and a keyboard, check that your monitor is plugged in and switched on, and press the on/off case switch to start the system. Now place the Windows XP CD in your CD/DVD drive and turn the computer off and back on again. As it restarts, BIOS will launch the Windows Setup program.

But first ...

What's the matter with SATA?

Bizarre though it may seem, and indeed is, there's a strong chance that you'll be unable to install Windows on a SATA hard disk. The trouble is that Windows won't recognise that the drive exists until you install a special SATA driver – and you can't install a special SATA driver because it is not on the Windows installation CD. The workaround is to copy the required driver from the CD supplied with your motherboard to a floppy disk and then install them at a critical juncture during installation. Of course, to transfer the driver from CD to floppy you'll need the use of another computer. You'll also need to follow the motherboard manual's instructions clearly. In our case, the relevant driver was stored in a folder called BootDrv which you wouldn't necessarily find without instructions. We then had to double-click an icon called MENU, select the appropriate chipset from a list in a DOS window, and finally copy the driver to the floppy.

If it's one step forward with SATA, it's two steps backwards with this nonsense. Don't think that you can copy the driver to a recordable CD, incidentally, as the Windows Setup routine will only search floppy disks for drivers.

Anyway, armed with your driver floppy, you can now install Windows. Just as it gets going, the setup program invites you to 'Press F6 if you need to install a third party SCSI or RAID driver'. This is your (misleading) cue. Hit F6, pop the floppy disk in its drive and follow the instructions.

The good news for some at least is that the latest chipsets make SATA drives look like normal IDE/ATA drives, in which case installation should proceed without a hiccup. We suggest that you try this first. If Windows refuses to install, follow the procedure just described – or, if your motherboard manual suggests otherwise, do what it says.

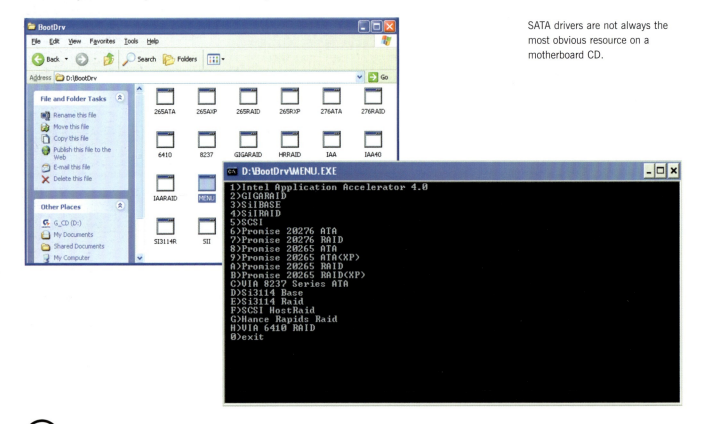

SATA drivers are not always the most obvious resource on a motherboard CD.

1

Plain text on an all-blue background isn't particularly user-friendly, but all that follows is straightforward. Press Enter to kick-start Setup into action.

```
Windows XP Home Edition Setup

Welcome to Setup.

This portion of the Setup program prepares Microsoft(R)
Windows(R) XP to run on your computer.

  • To set up Windows XP now, press ENTER.

  • To repair a Windows XP installation using
    Recovery Console, press R.

  • To quit Setup without installing Windows XP, press F3.

  ENTER=Continue   R=Repair   F3=Quit
```

2

The licence agreement. This is not the place to argue the merits or otherwise of your very limited rights as laid down by Microsoft. Besides which, you have no choice. Press F8 to accept the terms of engagement.

```
Windows XP Licensing Agreement

MICROSOFT WINDOWS XP HOME EDITION

END-USER LICENSE AGREEMENT FOR MICROSOFT
SOFTWARE

IMPORTANT-READ CAREFULLY: This End-User
License Agreement ("EULA") is a legal agreement between you
(either an individual or a single entity) and Microsoft
Corporation for the Microsoft software that accompanies this
EULA, which includes computer software and may include
associated media, printed materials, "online" or electronic
documentation, and Internet-based services ("Software"). An
amendment or addendum to this EULA may accompany the software.
YOU AGREE TO BE BOUND BY THE TERMS OF THIS
EULA BY INSTALLING, COPYING, OR OTHERWISE
USING THE SOFTWARE. IF YOU DO NOT AGREE, DO
NOT INSTALL, COPY, OR USE THE SOFTWARE; YOU
MAY RETURN IT TO YOUR PLACE OF PURCHASE FOR A
FULL REFUND, IF APPLICABLE.

1. GRANT OF LICENSE.  Microsoft grants you the following
   rights provided that you comply with all terms and
   conditions of this EULA:
   1.1 Installation and use.  You may install, use, access,
   display and run one copy of the Software on a single computer,
   such as a workstation, terminal or other device ("Workstation
   Computer").  The Software may not be used by more than one

 F8=I agree   ESC=I do not agree   PAGE DOWN=Next Page
```

3

You'll only see this screen if you're using an 'Upgrade' rather than a 'Full' version of XP. Microsoft discounts new releases of Windows to previous customers but you must prove that you have at some point owned a qualifying version. Pop an original Windows 2000, Millennium Edition, 98, 95 or NT CD in the drive now and press Enter. Don't worry about having to remove the XP disc in the meantime – you'll be prompted to return it shortly.

```
Windows XP Home Edition Setup

Setup cannot find a previous version of Windows installed on
your computer. To continue, Setup needs to verify that you
qualify to use this upgrade product.

Please insert one of the following Windows product CDs into the
CD-ROM drive: Windows XP Home Edition (full version),
Windows XP Professional (full version), Windows 2000 Professional,
Windows Millennium, Windows 98, Windows NT Workstation 4.0,
Windows 95, or Windows NT Workstation 3.51.

  • When the CD is in the drive, press ENTER.

  • To quit Setup, press F3.

  ENTER=Continue   F3=Quit
```

4

Setup will now ask you where you wish to install Windows. Assuming that you have a new, clean, unpartitioned hard disk, the default suggestion C: is correct. You will also be asked which file system you wish to use. Windows XP is designed for NTFS rather than FAT, so select NTFS and let Setup format the disk accordingly.

```
Windows XP Home Edition Setup

 The following list shows the existing partitions and
 unpartitioned space on this computer.

 Use the UP and DOWN ARROW keys to select an item in the list.

  • To set up Windows XP on the selected item, press ENTER.

  • To create a partition in the unpartitioned space, press C.

  • To delete the selected partition, press D.

 16379 MB Disk 0 at Id 0 on bus 0 on atapi [MBR]
    C:  Partition1 [FAT32]              16379 MB ( 16374 MB free)

  ENTER=Install   D=Delete Partition   F3=Quit
```

⑤

Setup will now ask you to replace the Windows XP CD in the drive, whereupon it copies the files it needs to the hard disk. Expect the system to reboot at the end of this process.

⑥

When your computer restarts, you will see a prompt inviting you to boot from the CD. However, this is rather misleading. Setup has already completed its first phase and can now boot straight from the hard disk. So do not press any keys, wait a minute and Setup will re-launch in a friendlier graphical guise.

⑦

Windows now installs. Your active involvement is required at a few stages, beginning with the Regional and Language settings. Click the Customise button and tell Windows where you live.

8

*Next, click the Details button and change the input language
and keyboard layout from US to UK (or whatever).*

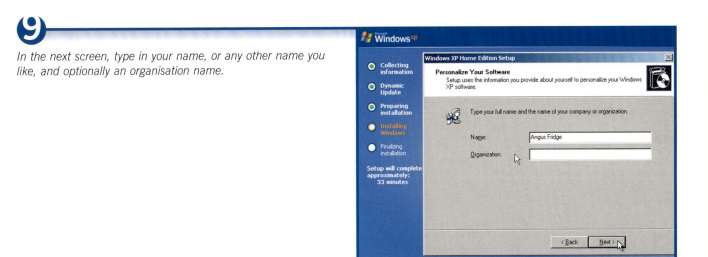

9

*In the next screen, type in your name, or any other name you
like, and optionally an organisation name.*

10

*Now enter the Windows XP Product Key. If you get it wrong,
which is easily done, Setup will refuse to continue until you get it
right.*

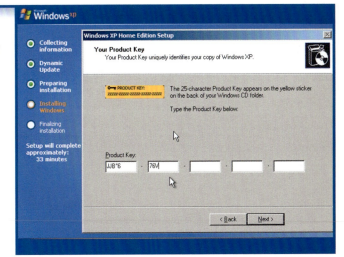

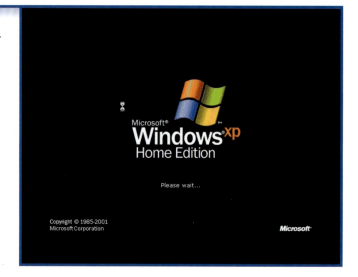

When prompted, give the computer its own name. This is essential for running a home network. In the next screen, accept the typical network settings.

Setup now runs merrily on for a while and can be safely ignored. At the end of this process, it reboots your computer. Again, be sure not to boot from the CD; let Setup boot from the hard disk instead. Eventually, Windows itself makes an appearance. All that remains is to follow a few final setup steps.

Chipset drivers

One of the first things Windows does is detect the presence of a monitor and load a default driver. It may also prompt you to install a driver supplied by the monitor manufacturer. You can do this now or later (check the manual for advice); what's important is that any Plug-and-Play monitor – and they're all Plug-and-Play these days – will work with Windows immediately.

Similarly, your AGP or PCI Express video card will function without any manual input but it will not live up to its potential until you install a dedicated driver.

In fact, the very first thing you should do is install the full set of chipset drivers from the CD supplied with the motherboard. This will bring your system fully up to speed and probably provide a couple of useful utilities.

QUICK Q&A

Now what?
Now install some strong antivirus software, enable the Windows firewall, sign up with an Internet Service Provider, pay a visit to the Windows Update website and download any critical patches, and otherwise take all the usual necessary steps to protect and secure your computer! We'll take it as read that you know what to do. After all, you *have* just built a computer from scratch.

PART 5 Installing a sound card

If you are not content with integrated audio or if your motherboard lacks such capability, you'll want to install a sound card. This can be installed in any PCI expansion slot. First, though, revisit the BIOS menu and disable the onboard audio chip.

You can disable your motherboard's integrated audio chip in the BIOS menu. Do this before installing a sound card. If you leave the setting on Auto, the motherboard should recognise the presence of a new card and turn off integrated audio automatically – but there's no guarantee.

Turn off your computer, unplug it from the mains and take the usual antistatic precautions. Open the computer case and lay it on its side. Now familiarise yourself with the layout of the expansion card (i.e. read the manual), decide which PCI slot to use and remove the corresponding blanking plate from the case. Remove the card from its antistatic bag and carefully install it in the expansion slot. Be sure not to touch any components. Secure the card to the case chassis with the screw.

2 Now connect the audio cables from your CD/DVD drives – but see the note on p.139 first.

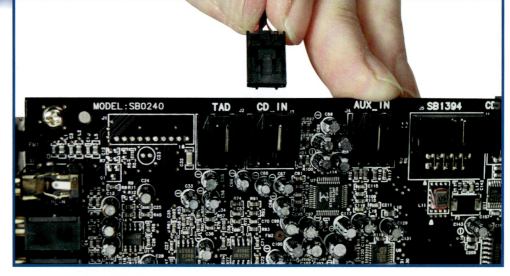

3 This card is supplied with an optional port bracket that supplies the computer with a MIDI/games port. It connects to the sound card by means of a cable. Note that a port bracket effectively blocks an expansion slot so you may prefer to live without one if slots are in short supply. With a small form factor case, you probably won't have the option to use a port bracket.

4 Remove a blanking plate and screw the port bracket into position next to the sound card. Finally, replace the computer covers, plug it in and fire it up. Windows will identify the new component and ask for a driver. Pop the supplied CD-ROM in the drive and follow the directions. You should also install any applications software shipped with the card and, of course, connect your speakers.

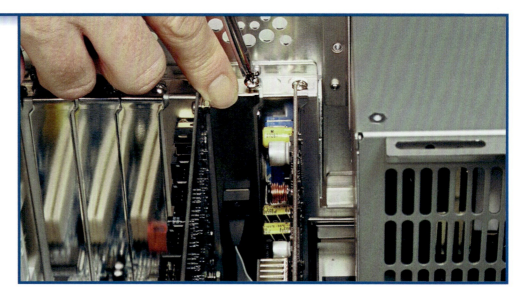

Digital audio extraction

We mentioned earlier (p.67) that many drives support digital audio extraction (DAE). With speakers connected to the sound card, this is the time to find out.

First, establish that you can hear an audio CD when played in the CD/DVD drive. Then check that DAE has been enabled within Windows. In Windows XP, click Start, Control Panel, Performance & Maintenance and System. This launches the System Properties window. Look in the Hardware tab and click Device Manager. Here you will find a list of all the hardware devices in your computer. Click the little '+' sign next to DVD/CD-ROM drives and then double-click the drive in question. In the Properties tab, ensure that the 'Enable digital CD audio for this CD-ROM device' box is checked (ticked). If this option is greyed-out and unclickable, the drive does not support DAE and you'll definitely need to use an audio cable. Repeat with the DVD drive.

Now turn off your computer, remove the covers and disconnect the audio cable from either the drive or the sound card. Reboot and try playing the CD again. If you still hear sound, you know that the drive supports DAE and you can remove the cable altogether.

Alternatively, of course, you can opt not to bother with internal audio cables in the first place and take a chance that DAE will work. That's what we do.

QUICK Q&A
How many PCI cards can I install?
As many as you have slots for on your motherboard. The PCI bus is natively 'Plug-and-Play', which means the computer can apportion system resources automatically and avoid hardware conflicts.

It's not such a huge deal, really, but Digital Audio Extraction lets you dispense with those fiddly internal sound cables. Anything that reduces the risk of cables snagging fans is welcome.

PART ⑤ Loose ends

You should now have a fully-functioning, home-built, better-than-off-the-shelf PC at your disposal. Congratulations – the hard work is done! If everything is behaving as it should, now is the time to consider further hardware installations to complete the picture.

In a mid-tower case such as this it's not always easy to clear away extraneous clutter. Just ensure that cables are kept well away from fans and check that airflow in and out of the case is not blocked. Here, the sound card's bracket cable is rather too close to the video card's heatsink.

There is one final, rather pressing matter to take care of, namely tidying your PC's interior. The trouble here is that there's no 'right' way to do it as such; it's really just a matter of bunching together surplus power cables and tucking them out of the way … somewhere. A free drive bay is fine. Keep dangling cables away from fans and other components, and ensure that, so far as possible, cables do not impede airflow through the case. Your computer case manufacturer may have included a few plastic cable ties, or else you can use your own. Avoid metal ties, even if coated in paper or plastic, as these could short-circuit the motherboard. Again, the benefits of a tall tower case with plenty of room are apparent, but even a mid- or mini-tower can be kept reasonably tidy.

A full-tower case is a cinch to keep tidy. This example is further helped by the use of round IDE/ATA cables instead of the usual flat ribbon cables and a side-mounted hard disk drive.

PART 5 Imaging the hard disk

The moment you have your computer up and running with the chipset drivers installed and Windows (or any other operating system) at the helm, we suggest that you make a global system-wide backup. The reason for this is to give yourself a failsafe checkpoint to which you can return should anything, or everything, go awry.

Think of a worst case scenario in which your main or sole hard disk drive suffers hardware failure, or a scenario almost as bleak where your Windows installation becomes corrupt to the point of uselessness, perhaps following a virus infection. If you make a disk image now, you will always be able to return to this point in the future, even if you have to install a fresh hard disk.

Of course, you should also make regular backups on a daily or weekly basis to minimise the risk of losing precious files. But for now, we're concerned solely with a last-gasp back-to-square-one backup that may one day save you having to reinstall Windows, motherboard and hardware drivers all over again.

You can store a drive image on the original hard disk, on a second hard disk, or to a different computer over a network. For the easiest possible disaster recovery, we recommend that you use a second hard drive – which is why, in fact, we installed two drives in our tower case. As well as providing additional storage space, the second drive makes a perfect home for an image of the primary drive.

If you have only one hard drive, as in our small form factor PC, you can partition it into two or more distinct chunks and save your image file on a different partition from the C: drive (i.e. the partition on which Windows is installed). This is almost as good as having two drives with the obvious drawback that you won't be able to access a saved image if the drive physically malfunctions.

Alternatively again, you can save an image of your hard drive directly to recordable CD or DVD media. Label these discs carefully and store them somewhere safe and away from the computer. Better still, do both: save the image file to a second hard disk *and* copy it to CD/DVD.

In this example, we'll use Norton Ghost from Symantec (**www.symantec.com**).

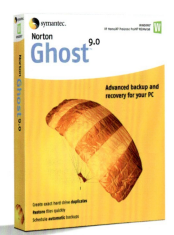

Norton Ghost is one of the most popular disk-imaging tools.

1

Install Norton Ghost and reboot when prompted.

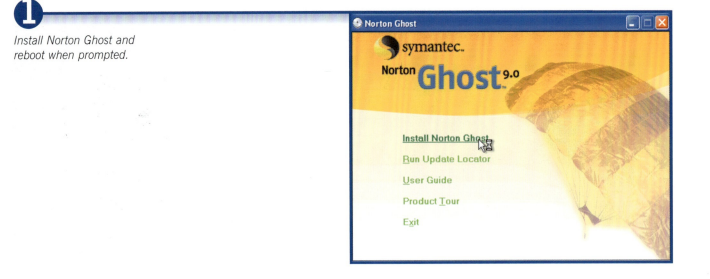

The first time you launch the program, you will be prompted to install Microsoft .Net framework. This provides a special working environment within which Ghost can operate. It takes a while but it's not optional.

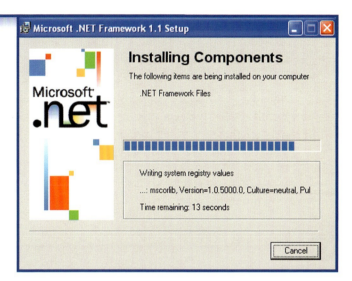

Next, you will be asked to unlock the program with the serial code provided. This done, you can finally launch Ghost ready for action. This is a good time to follow the built-in tutorials in the Learn About section.

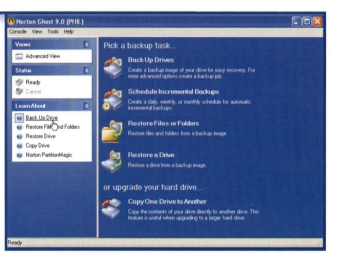

When you're ready, click Back Up Drives in the Pick a backup task section. This launches the Drive Backup Wizard. Click Next.

5

Now select the hard drive that you wish to back up. This will usually be C: drive.

6

Decide where you want the disk image to be saved. For this first backup, we will use our recordable drive so select the CD-RW/DVD-RW option. Alternatively, you could save the image to the primary or a second hard disk. If you select Local file here, Ghost offers an option to split the image file into convenient CD or DVD-sized chunks, which makes it easy to copy the backup to removable media later.

7

Put a blank recordable CD or DVD in your drive, click the Browse button, and select the appropriate drive. Click Next.

Ghost now asks you whether you wish to compress the image. Accept Standard and check the box to verify the image after creation.

Click Next twice to start the backup. The beauty of Ghost is that it can image the C: drive from within Windows. However, the less you do while a backup is in progress, the better.

10

If the first disc fills up before the image is complete, Ghost simply prompts for a second disc and spans the image over as many discs as it takes. You can now use these discs to restore the drive. How?

11

In two ways. If you can start Windows and run Ghost, you can initiate a restore procedure very easily using the Restore Drive Wizard from the main program menu. Point the program to the first disc and the rest is pretty much automatic.

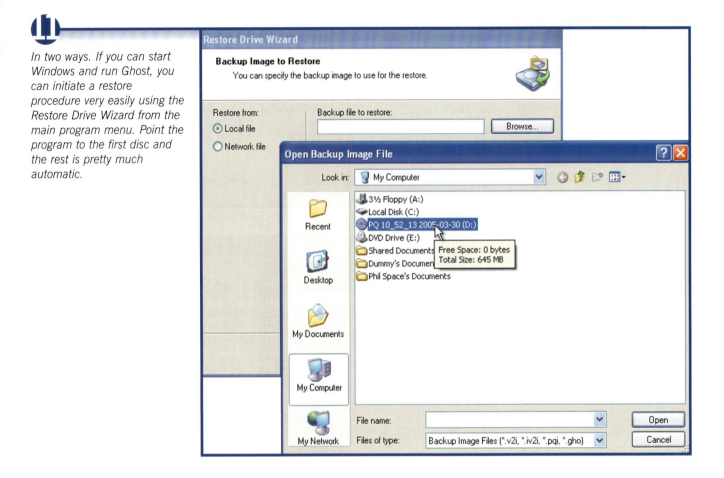

12

If you cannot start the computer normally, you can use the Ghost CD as a boot disc. Ensure that your CD/DVD drive is listed as the first boot device in BIOS (see p.130) and restart with the Ghost CD in the drive. This launches the Recovery Environment.

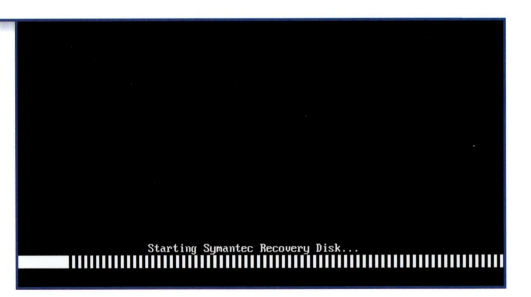

13

*Click Advanced Recovery
Tasks and then System
Restore. This launches the
System Restore Wizard.*

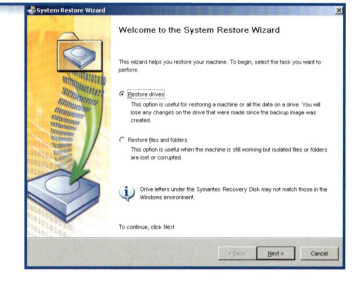

14

*Now point the wizard to your image file or to the first disc in a
spanned series. See Quick Q&A box for help here. The wizard
will now restore your drive to its original condition.*

?

QUICK Q&A

**Hang on a second. Isn't there a flaw with this system recovery
business?**
Yes, sometimes. The problem relates to Steps 12–14. If you only have one
CD/DVD drive in your system and your backup is on CD or DVD, you have a
dilemma. If you boot the computer with the Ghost CD, you cannot then
remove that CD from the drive and replace it with the first of your backup
discs in Step 14. If you try, the Ghost recovery program will simply halt. What
you need is either a second CD or DVD drive in your computer or access to a
networked computer that holds a copy of your image files (Ghost supports
system recovery across most networks). Alternatively, if you saved your
image file to a second hard disk rather than to CD/DVD media, you can
restore from there now. This is what we recommend.

PART ⑤ Troubleshooting

Let's assume you've built your PC, turned it on for the first time … and nothing happens. You can't get into BIOS, let alone install Windows. How and where do you begin to trouble-shoot?

In fact, identifying a problem at this stage is very much easier than down the road when you've got a printer, scanner, webcam and goodness knows what other hardware attached; not to mention 57 software programs doing their utmost to interfere with one another, a real risk of viruses and perhaps a utility suite that does more harm than good. Your computer will never be so easy to diagnose and cure as it is right now.

Check the cables

The very first step is all too obvious but all too often overlooked: check that all external cables are securely connected in the correct places:

- [ ] The computer's PSU should be plugged into a mains wall socket (or power gangplank).
- [ ] So should the monitor.
- [ ] The mains electricity supply should be turned on at the wall.
- [ ] The monitor should be connected to the video card's VGA or DVI output.
- [ ] The keyboard should be connected to the computer's PS/2-style keyboard port (not to a USB port, unless USB support has already been enabled in BIOS, and not to the mouse port).
- [ ] The PSU should be set to the correct voltage and turned on.

Now turn on the monitor. A power indication LED on the monitor housing should illuminate and, hopefully, you'll see something on the screen. If not, re-read the monitor manual and double-check that you've correctly identified the on/off switch and are not busy fiddling with the brightness or contrast controls. It's not always obvious which switch is which. If the power light still does not come on, it sounds like the monitor itself may be at fault. Try changing the fuse in the cable. Ideally, test the monitor with another PC.

Internal inspection

Now turn on the PC itself. Press the large on/off switch on the front of the case, not the smaller reset switch. You should hear the whirring of internal fans and either a single or a sequence of beeps. But let's assume that all seems lifeless. Again, check/change the fuse in the PSU power cable. If this doesn't help, unplug all cables, including the monitor, take off the case covers and lay the computer on its side. Now systematically check every internal connection. Again, here's a quick checklist to tick off:

- ☐ PSU should be connected to the motherboard with a large 24-pin plug and also, if appropriate, with ATX 12V and ATX Auxiliary cables.
- ☐ The heatsink fan should be plugged into a power socket on the motherboard.
- ☐ The case fans should be likewise connected.
- ☐ All drives should be connected to the appropriate sockets on the motherboard with ribbon cables.
- ☐ All drives should be connected to the PSU with power cables.
- ☐ The video card should be securely sited in its AGP or PCI Express slot.
- ☐ All other expansion cards should be likewise in place.
- ☐ Look for loose screws inside the case, lest one should be causing a short-circuit.
- ☐ If your motherboard has jumpers, check that they are correctly set.
- ☐ Check the front panel connections. If the case's on/off switch is disconnected from the motherboard, you won't be able to start the system.
- ☐ Are any cables snagging on fans?
- ☐ Double-check that Pin 1 positions on cables and drives are correctly matched (confession time: we initially got this wrong with the un-keyed floppy drive cable plug).
- ☐ Are the retention clips on the memory DIMMs fully closed?
- ☐ Does anything on the motherboard look obviously broken or damaged?

Disconnect each cable in turn and look for bent pins on the plugs and sockets. These can usually be straightened with small, pointy pliers and a steady hand. Reconnect everything, including the monitor and power cable, and turn the computer on once more. Leave the covers off to aid observation. Does it now burst into life as if by magic? Rather gallingly, unplugging and replacing a cable is sometimes all it takes to fix an elusive but strictly temporary glitch.

PSU problems

Look for an LED on the motherboard (check the manual for its location). This should illuminate whenever the PSU is connected to the mains power and turned on, even when the computer itself is off. The LED confirms that the motherboard is receiving power; if it stays dark, the PSU itself may be at fault.

When you turn on the computer, do the fans remain static? Does the CD drive disc tray refuse to open? Is all depressingly dead? This would confirm the PSU as the problem. Use an alternative power cable, perhaps borrowed from the monitor, just to be sure. If still nothing happens, remove and replace the PSU.

NEVER TRY TO OPEN OR REPAIR A PSU. Nor should you try running it while it's disconnected from the motherboard, as a PSU can only operate with a load.

Next steps

Let's assume that there is evidence of power flowing to the motherboard: the LED comes on and the heatsink and case fans spin. The PSU must be okay but there's still nothing on the monitor screen. Did you hear a beep as the computer powered up? This is a good thing. A sequence of beeps is generally a sign – a welcome sign, in fact – of specific, identifiable trouble. See the Power On Self Test (POST) section on p.151.

Check the keyboard. If anything is resting on the keys, remove it. This alone can cause a computer to pause. As the computer powers up, three lights on the keyboard should illuminate within the first few seconds. If they fail to do so, it's just possible that a dud keyboard is responsible for halting the entire system. Disconnect it and reboot the computer without a keyboard attached. If you now see a keyboard error message on the monitor screen where all was blank before, it looks like you need a new one. Connect an alternative keyboard to the computer and reboot again to confirm the diagnosis.

Another clue: if the computer partially boots but then stalls, check the memory count during the POST procedure. If the RAM total differs from the memory you installed, it looks like you have a DIMM problem to deal with. Remove, clean and replace each module. If that gets you nowhere, try booting with a single module in place, and experiment with each in turn. Check the motherboard manual for details here; a single module must usually be installed in a specific DIMM slot (usually DIMM1). If you can start the computer successfully at some point, you should be able to identify and exclude faulty modules. This isn't much help if you only have one module, of course.

Back to basics

Failing all of the above, disconnect all power and ribbon cables from the drives and the motherboard. Unplug and remove the video card and any other expansion cards, disconnect the case fans and leave only a single memory module in place. In short, reduce the system to a bare bones configuration where the only remaining connections are between the PSU and the motherboard: ATX power, ATA Auxiliary and ATX 12V. Do not

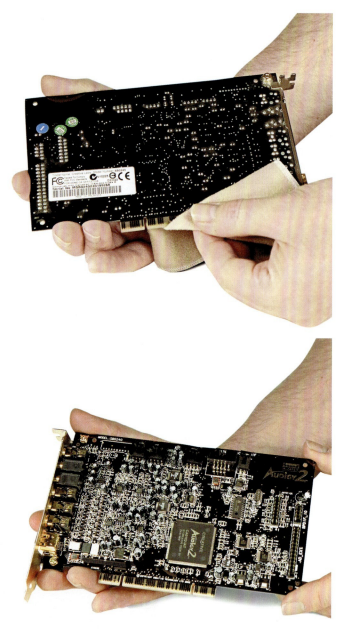

When handling expansion cards, be very careful not to touch either their onboard components or the lower gold connecting edge. With a card out of its slot, take the opportunity to clean its connecting edge with a lint-free cloth.

remove the heatsink or processor and leave all the front panel connections in place.

Now turn on the power once more. You should hear some diagnostic beeps from the BIOS. If so, see the following POST section and Appendix 3. If not, check the speaker connection.

If that doesn't resolve matters, turn off the computer, remove the power cable, and gradually, carefully, step-by-step, put it all back together again. Begin with the video card. Connect a monitor you know to be working and reboot the system. This will give you the added benefit of being able to read any onscreen error messages as you go along. If the screen stays blank, you know for sure that the video card is at fault. Replace it.

Reconnect a functioning keyboard next. Reboot and check that your computer gets past POST – i.e. that you can successfully enter the BIOS Setup routine. Now reconnect the floppy drive ribbon and power cables and reboot once more. Reinstall the hard disk drive next, followed by the CD and DVD drives. Every step of the way, reboot the computer and ensure that it doesn't hang or abort during POST. At some point, the computer may refuse to start – and right there you will have identified your problem. Alternatively, it may start normally all the way through and you may never find out what the original stumbling block was. No matter: either way, you have successfully solved your hardware hassles.

Power On Self Test (POST)

The very first thing a computer does when it starts is give itself a quick once-over to check that it still has a processor, memory and motherboard. If this POST procedure finds a serious problem, or 'fatal error', it is likely to throw a wobbly and halt the computer in its tracks. That's the assumption we have been working on in this section.

However, it also gives you two useful diagnostic clues (actually three, but hexadecimal checkpoint codes are beyond the scope of this book).

First, assuming that the video card and monitor are both working, you should see some onscreen error messages. These may be self-explanatory or relatively obscure, depending on the problem and the BIOS manufacturer, but should offer at least some help. A memory error would indicate that one or more of your modules is either faulty or not properly installed; a 'hard disk not found' message would most likely point to a loose connection or perhaps a faulty IDE/ATA cable.

Secondly, so long as the case speaker is connected (see p.96), the motherboard will emit a series of POST-generated beeps. These can help you identify the specific component causing the problem.

We list some common beep code and error messages in Appendix 3.

POST is a low-key but essential routine that the computer runs through before launching Windows or any other operating system. Keep an eye out for error messages on the screen and an ear out for beep codes.

```
CPU ID/ucod : 0F34                    Extended Memory  :   2047M
CPU Clock   : 3.40GHz                 Cache Memory     :     1M

Diskette Drive A : 1.44M, 3.5"        Display Type      : EGA/VGA
Diskette Drive B : None               Serial Port(s)    : 3F8 2F8
Pri. Master Disk : DVD-RW,ATA 66      Parallel Port(s)  : 378
Pri. Slave  Disk : None               DDR2 at Bank(s)   : 0 1 4 5
Sec. Master Disk : None
Sec. Slave  Disk : None
```

```
PCI Devices Listing ...
Bus  Dev  Fun  Vendor  Device  SVID  SSID  Class  Device Class              IRQ

 0    29   0    8086    2658   1458  2658  0C03   USB 1.1 Host Cntrlr        12
 0    29   1    8086    2659   1458  2659  0C03   USB 1.1 Host Cntrlr        11
 0    29   2    8086    265A   1458  265A  0C03   USB 1.1 Host Cntrlr         5
 0    29   3    8086    265B   1458  265A  0C03   USB 1.1 Host Cntrlr        10
 0    31   1    8086    266F   1458  266F  0101   IDE Cntrlr                 14
 0    31   2    8086    2652   1458  B002  0101   Native IDE Cntrlr          11
 0    31   3    8086    266A   1458  266A  0C05   SMBus Cntrlr               11
 1     0   0    1002    5E4D   1458  2106  0300   Display Cntrlr             10
                                                  ACPI Controller            9

Boot from CD :
DISK BOOT FAILURE, INSERT SYSTEM DISK AND PRESS ENTER
```

SAMSUNG   SyncMaster 151s

6

PART **6** # Appendices

Appendix 1
Silence is golden … well, copper and aluminium

If there is one thing the average desktop computer is not, it is quiet. Gallingly, the more high-powered you make it, the noisier it becomes. It all boils down to the cooling systems inside the case, i.e. a bunch of low-tech fans. There are fans in the PSU, fans built into the case, a fan on the processor heatsink, probably another on the Northbridge chip and yet another on the video card. Combined, they make a racket that's loud enough to be off-putting at best and to drown out music or game soundtracks at worst.

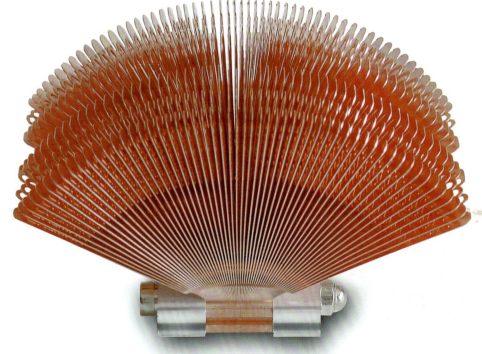

Freaky-looking it may be but this completely-silent Zalman 'Flower Cooler' can replace a boisterous CPU heatsink. All it needs is a really big, really quiet fan to supply it with fresh air.

However, there are some useful counter-measures available and here the DIY system builder can customise a computer to suit. For one, consider a passive heatsink for the processor, i.e. one without a powered fan. There are plenty of bizarre-looking but highly-effective heatsinks around that can keep the processor well within acceptable temperature limitations (under 75° Celsius for a Pentium 4).

Even chipset fans tend to be irritatingly intrusive, so you might care to remove the Northbridge heatsink and replace it with a silent fan-less alternative.

Most recent video cards also use fan-assisted heatsinks to cool the GPU. Here again it is often possible to replace the original with a silent version. Be careful, though: some of the latest video chips run so hot that a passive heatsink alone is not sufficient unless there is also a fan nearby to supply cool air.

There's little to do about a noisy PSU other than replace it with a quiet one – or, of course, to buy a quiet PSU in the first place. Check the specs and look for an acoustic noise level of about 30dB when the unit is running at 75% capacity.

Going further, you can even encase the hard disk drive in an acoustic enclosure and clad the interior of the case with sound-muffling panels.

Cooling caveats

Just a couple:

1. In smaller cases, the PSU is often located directly above the processor socket (as, in fact, in our project – see p.94). This generally rules out a passive heatsink because there simply isn't the necessary clearance over the processor. And even if you can squeeze one into the available space, don't forget that …

2. Even an elaborate super-effective passive heatsink needs some independent cooling. This is generally provided by a large, variable-speed ultra-quiet fan positioned directly above the heatsink and held in place with an angled bracket attached to the case. Again, this is not possible in most mid-tower cases.

In short, don't shell out for an inventive cooling solution unless you're sure your case can accommodate it. If you have an unobstructed view of the processor socket when the motherboard and PSU are both in place inside the case, you should be OK.

Consult Quiet PC for specialist advice and products, including the Zalman range of silent heatsinks (see Appendix 4).

If your chipset has a fan, consider replacing it with an efficient passive heatsink. So long as there is reasonable airflow inside the case, this will keep it cool and quiet.

If even the clicking of the hard disk drive drives you to distraction, encase your case in mufflers.

A silent copper-finned heatsink fitted to a video card cuts out one source of noise completely.

PART 6

Appendix 2
A home entertainment PC?

A computer in your living room is the future, you know. No, really!

Although you may not appreciate it, the computer you build with the help of this book could, with only a couple of tweaks and a cable to connect it to your TV, make a stunning home entertainment centre. We're talking about:

- A digital recorder that records analogue and/or digital TV channels, with full scheduling facilities provided by an electronic programme guide (EPG) and the ability to pause live TV
- A DVD player
- A music centre that plays audio CD and MP3 (and similar) music files
- An audio recorder that copies CDs
- The benefits of a multi-channel surround sound speaker system
- A showcase for your digital images, with special effects, videos and slideshows
- A radio
- Games playing
- Remote control

And it's *still* a full-blown Windows XP computer!

All this and more is possible if you install a TV tuner card in your system, subscribe to an EPG service and use the right software. By far the easiest approach is using Windows Media Center Edition 2005, which is basically a version of Windows XP customised for home entertainment.

Does this look like your home? Never mind – you can still use a PC as the hub of your home entertainment system.

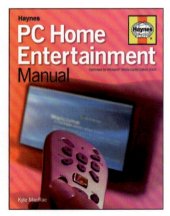

All you need to know about domesticating a computer.

This is an off-the-shelf Media Center PC but you can just as easily build your own. Note the digital TV tuner card, which is all you need to receive Freeview channels.

It used to be impossible to build your own Media Center computer, as Microsoft only released the operating system to original equipment manufacturers (OEMs). That meant that if you wanted a home entertainment PC, you had to buy one off the shelf – and that, given that you've bought this book, is not going to appeal to you.

It is now possible to buy the 2005 version of Media Center as a standalone operating system provided you buy at least one bit of hardware with it. This technically turns you into an OEM. Microsoft's support for this sales route seems sketchy but the reality is that you go out and buy, say, a Media Center-compatible remote control and thus qualify to buy Media Center software at the same time.

What's to stop you building your own Media Center PC? Nothing at all, frankly, and we'd certainly suggest that you give it careful consideration. A barebones kit like the Shuttle system we used earlier is ideal for a home entertainment computer, and would look just at home tucked under a telly as perched on a desk. However, it is important to emphasise that Media Center software will not work with just any old combination of hardware. You have to be particularly careful to choose a compatible TV

tuner and you'll certainly want a remote control. Unless and until Microsoft gets its act together and actively markets Media Center to non-commercial system builders, this means a bit of legwork and a little uncertainty.

The best advice we can offer is to go to the Green Button, **www.thegreenbutton.com**. This is an unofficial site run by and for Media Center enthusiasts and you'll find everything you need to know about workable hardware combinations. Drop by before you go shopping!

Also check out Media Center's official UK home at **www.microsoft.com/uk/windowsxp/mediacenter**.

And if you want to learn more about the possibilities, whether using Media Center or alternative software, get hold of the Haynes *PC Home Entertainment Manual*.

Some shops will send you the Media Center Edition 2005 operating system if you buy a Media Center remote control unit.

A small form factor Media Center PC looks at home in the lounge.

PART ⑥ Appendix 3 Beep and error codes

As we discussed on p.97 and p.151, the motherboard – or more precisely, the BIOS chip on the motherboard – emits a sequence of beeps whenever it identifies a problem that is serious enough to prevent the computer from starting normally. If the BIOS does manage to get the computer up and running, it can also generate onscreen error messages that help you identify trouble spots. Here we reprint the codes used by AMI and Award, makers of two commonly used BIOS programs.

Phoenix, another major player, uses a rather more complicated scheme that is beyond our scope here.

AMI BIOS beep codes

Number of Beeps	Problem	Action
1	Memory refresh timer error.	Remove each memory module, clean the connecting edge that plugs into the motherboard socket, and replace. If that doesn't work, try restarting with a single memory module and see if you can identify the culprit by a process of elimination. If you still get the error code, replace with known good modules.
2	Parity error.	As with 1 beep above.
3	Main memory read/write test error.	As with 1 beep above.
4	Motherboard timer not operational.	Either the motherboard is faulty or one of the expansion cards has a problem. Remove all cards except the video card and restart. If the motherboard still issues this beep code, it has a serious, probably fatal problem. If the beeps stop, replace the cards one at a time and restart each time. This should identify the guilty party.
5	Processor error.	As with 4 beeps above.
6	Keyboard controller BAT test error.	As with 4 beeps above.
7	General exception error.	As with 4 beeps above.
8	Display memory error.	The video card is missing, faulty or incorrectly installed. Remove, clean the connecting contacts and replace. If that doesn't work, try using a different video card. If you are using integrated video instead of a video card, the motherboard may be faulty.
9	ROM checksum error.	As with 4 beeps above.
10	CMOS shutdown register read/write error.	As with 4 beeps above.
11	Cache memory bad.	As with 4 beeps above.

AMIBIOS8 Checkpoint and Beep Code List version 1.2. Copyright of American Megatrends, Inc. Reprinted with permission. All rights reserved.

AMI BIOS error codes Here are some examples of onscreen error messages:

Error	Action
Gate20 Error	The BIOS is unable to properly control the motherboard's Gate A20 function, which controls access of memory over 1MB. This may indicate a problem with the motherboard.
Multi-Bit ECC Error	This message will only occur on systems using ECC-enabled memory modules. ECC memory has the ability to correct single-bit errors that may occur from faulty memory modules. A multiple bit corruption of memory has occurred, and the ECC memory algorithm cannot correct it. This may indicate a defective memory module.
Parity Error	Fatal Memory Parity Error. System halts after displaying this message.
Boot Failure	This is a generic message indicating the BIOS could not boot from a particular device. This message is usually followed by other information concerning the device.
Invalid Boot Diskette	A diskette was found in the drive, but it is not configured as a bootable diskette.
Drive Not Ready	The BIOS was unable to access the drive because it indicated it was not ready for data transfer. This is often reported by drives when no media is present.
A: Drive Error	The BIOS attempted to configure the A: drive during POST, but was unable to properly configure the device. This may be because of a bad cable or faulty diskette drive.
Insert BOOT diskette in A:	The BIOS attempted to boot from the A: drive, but could not find a proper boot diskette.
Reboot and Select proper Boot device or Insert Boot Media in selected Boot device	BIOS could not find a bootable device in the system and/or removable media drive does not contain media.
NO ROM BASIC	This message occurs on some systems when no bootable device can be detected.
Primary Master Hard Disk Error	The IDE/ATAPI device configured as Primary Master could not be properly initialized by the BIOS. This message is typically displayed when the BIOS is trying to detect and configure IDE/ATAPI devices in POST.
Primary Slave Hard Disk Error	The IDE/ATAPI device configured as Primary Slave could not be properly initialized by the BIOS. This message is typically displayed when the BIOS is trying to detect and configure IDE/ATAPI devices in POST.
Secondary Master Hard Disk Error	The IDE/ATAPI device configured as Secondary Master could not be properly initialized by the BIOS. This message is typically displayed when the BIOS is trying to detect and configure IDE/ATAPI devices in POST.
Secondary Slave Hard Disk Error	The IDE/ATAPI device configured as Secondary Slave could not be properly initialized by the BIOS. This message is typically displayed when the BIOS is trying to detect and configure IDE/ATAPI devices in POST.

AMI BIOS error codes continued:

Error	Action
Primary Master Drive – ATAPI Incompatible	The IDE/ATAPI device configured as Primary Master failed an ATAPI compatibility test. This message is typically displayed when the BIOS is trying to detect and configure IDE/ATAPI devices in POST.
Primary Slave Drive – ATAPI Incompatible	The IDE/ATAPI device configured as Primary Slave failed an ATAPI compatibility test. This message is typically displayed when the BIOS is trying to detect and configure IDE/ATAPI devices in POST.
Secondary Master Drive – ATAPI Incompatible	The IDE/ATAPI device configured as Secondary Master failed an ATAPI compatibility test. This message is typically displayed when the BIOS is trying to detect and configure IDE/ATAPI devices in POST.
Secondary Slave Drive – ATAPI Incompatible	The IDE/ATAPI device configured as Secondary Slave failed an ATAPI compatibility test. This message is typically displayed when the BIOS is trying to detect and configure IDE/ATAPI devices in POST.
S.M.A.R.T. Capable but Command Failed	The BIOS tried to send a S.M.A.R.T. message to a hard disk, but the command transaction failed. This message can be reported by an ATAPI device using the S.M.A.R.T. error reporting standard. S.M.A.R.T. failure messages may indicate the need to replace the hard disk.
S.M.A.R.T. Command Failed	The BIOS tried to send a S.M.A.R.T. message to a hard disk, but the command transaction failed. This message can be reported by an ATAPI device using the S.M.A.R.T. error reporting standard. S.M.A.R.T. failure messages may indicate the need to replace the hard disk.
S.M.A.R.T. Status BAD, Backup and Replace	A S.M.A.R.T. capable hard disk sends this message when it detects an imminent failure. This message can be reported by an ATAPI device using the S.M.A.R.T. error reporting standard. S.M.A.R.T. failure messages may indicate the need to replace the hard disk.
S.M.A.R.T. Capable and Status BAD	A S.M.A.R.T. capable hard disk sends this message when it detects an imminent failure. This message can be reported by an ATAPI device using the S.M.A.R.T. error reporting standard. S.M.A.R.T. failure messages may indicate the need to replace the hard disk.
BootSector Write!!	The BIOS has detected software attempting to write to a drive's boot sector. This is flagged as possible virus activity. This message will only be displayed if Virus Detection is enabled in AMIBIOS Setup.
VIRUS: Continue (Y/N)?	If the BIOS detects possible virus activity, it will prompt the user. This message will only be displayed if Virus Detection is enabled in AMIBIOS Setup.
DMA-2 Error	Error initializing secondary DMA controller. This is a fatal error, often indicating a problem with system hardware.
DMA Controller Error	POST error while trying to initialize the DMA controller. This is a fatal error, often indicating a problem with system hardware.

AMI BIOS error codes continued:

Error	Action
CMOS Date/Time Not Set	The CMOS Date and/or Time are invalid. This error can be resolved by readjusting the system time in AMIBIOS Setup.
CMOS Battery Low	CMOS Battery is low. This message usually indicates that the CMOS battery needs to be replaced. It could also appear when the user intentionally discharges the CMOS battery.
CMOS Settings Wrong	CMOS settings are invalid. This error can be resolved by using AMIBIOS Setup.
CMOS Checksum Bad	CMOS contents failed the Checksum check. Indicates that the CMOS data has been changed by a program other than the BIOS or that the CMOS is not retaining its data due to malfunction. This error can typically be resolved by using AMIBIOS Setup.
Keyboard Error	Keyboard is not present or the hardware is not responding when the keyboard controller is initialized.
Keyboard/Interface Error	Keyboard Controller failure. This may indicate a problem with system hardware.
System Halted	The system has been halted. A reset or power cycle is required to reboot the machine. This message appears after a fatal error has been detected.

Award BIOS beep codes

Number of Beeps	Problem	Action
1 long beep followed by 2 short beeps	Video card problem	Remove the card, clean the connecting edge that plugs into the motherboard socket, and replace. If that doesn't work, try an alternative video card to establish whether the problem lies with the card or the AGP slot. If you are using integrated video instead of a video card, the motherboard may be faulty.
Any other beeps	Memory problem	Remove each memory module, clean the connecting edge that plugs into the motherboard socket, and replace. If that doesn't work, try restarting with a single memory module and see if you can identify the culprit by a process of elimination. If you still get the error code, replace with known good modules.

Award BIOS error codes Here are the standard Award onscreen error messages:

Error	Action
BIOS ROM checksum error – System halted	The checksum of the BIOS code in the BIOS chip is incorrect, indicating the BIOS code may have become corrupt. Contact your system dealer to replace the BIOS.
CMOS battery failed	The CMOS battery is no longer functional. Contact your system dealer for a replacement battery.
CMOS checksum error – Defaults loaded	Checksum of CMOS is incorrect, so the system loads the default equipment configuration. A checksum error may indicate that CMOS has become corrupt. This error may have been caused by a weak battery. Check the battery and replace if necessary.
CPU at nnnn	Displays the running speed of the CPU.
Display switch is set incorrectly	The display switch on the motherboard can be set to either monochrome or colour. This message indicates the switch is set to a different setting from that indicated in Setup. Determine which setting is correct, and then either turn off the system and change the jumper, or enter Setup and change the VIDEO selection.
Press ESC to skip memory test	The user may press Esc to skip the full memory test.
Floppy disk(s) fail	Cannot find or initialize the floppy drive controller or the drive. Make sure the controller is installed correctly. If no floppy drives are installed, be sure the Diskette Drive selection in Setup is set to NONE or AUTO.
HARD DISK initializing. Please wait a moment.	Some hard drives require extra time to initialize.
HARD DISK INSTALL FAILURE	Cannot find or initialize the hard drive controller or the drive. Make sure the controller is installed correctly. If no hard drives are installed, be sure the Hard Drive selection in Setup is set to NONE.
Hard disk(s) diagnosis fail	The system may run specific disk diagnostic routines. This message appears if one or more hard disks return an error when the diagnostics run.
Keyboard error or no keyboard present	Cannot initialize the keyboard. Make sure the keyboard is attached correctly and no keys are pressed during POST. To purposely configure the system without a keyboard, set the error halt condition in Setup to HALT ON ALL, BUT KEYBOARD. The BIOS then ignores the missing keyboard during POST.
Keyboard is locked out – Unlock the key	This message usually indicates that one or more keys have been pressed during the keyboard tests. Be sure no objects are resting on the keyboard.
Memory Test	This message displays during a full memory test, counting down the memory areas being tested.
Memory test fail	If POST detects an error during memory testing, additional information appears giving specifics about the type and location of the memory error.
Override enabled – Defaults loaded	If the system cannot boot using the current CMOS configuration, the BIOS can override the current configuration with a set of BIOS defaults designed for the most stable, minimal-performance system operations.
Press TAB to show POST screen	System OEMs may replace the Phoenix Technologies' AwardBIOS POST display with their own proprietary display. Including this message in the OEM display permits the operator to switch between the OEM display and the default POST display.
Primary master hard disk fail	POST detects an error in the primary master IDE hard drive.
Primary slave hard disk fail	POST detects an error in the secondary master IDE hard drive.
Secondary master hard disk fail	POST detects an error in the primary slave IDE hard drive.
Secondary slave hard disk fail	POST detects an error in the secondary slave IDE hard drive.

Appendix 4
Further resources

Here are some useful links that will lead you to more detailed information on selected subjects.

High Street retailers

Maplin	www.maplin.co.uk
PC World	www.pcworld.co.uk

Web/mail order retailers

Dabs	www.dabs.com/uk
Bosse Computers	www.bossecomputers.com
Tekheads	www.tekheads.co.uk
Overclockers	www.overclockers.co.uk
Quiet PC	www.quietpc.com/uk

Computer fair contacts

Computer Fairs Information	www.computerfairs.co.uk
Northern Computer Markets	www.computermarkets.co.uk
Computer Markets Online	www.computermarketsonline.co.uk
The Show Guide	www.theshowguide.co.uk
All-Formats Computer Fairs	www.afm96.co.uk
The Best Event	www.bestevent.co.uk
Abacus Computer Fairs	www.fairs.co.uk

B-grade retailers

Morgan Computers	www.morgancomputers.co.uk
Dabs	www.dabs.com/uk/channels/Usedclearance
IT Dealers	www.itdealers.co.uk/catalog/index.php

High street and web retailers also sell-off B-grade stock from time to time; look for bargain bins, manager's specials and the like.

Consumer rights information

Trading Standards Institute	www.tradingstandards.gov.uk
Office of Fair Trading	www.oft.gov.uk

Processor manufacturers

Intel	www.intel.com
AMD	www.amd.com

Chipset information

Intel	www.intel.com
AMD	www.amd.com
ALi	www.ali.com.tw
VIA	www.via.com.tw
SiS	www.sis.com
Nvidia	www.nvidia.com

Intel and AMD also publish lists of motherboards that are compatible with their processors:

Intel	http://indigo.intel.com/mbsg/
AMD	http://snipurl.com/drwp

Memory information

Crucial Technology	http://support.crucial.com
Kingston Technology	www.kingston.com/ukroot
Rambus	www.rambus.com

Utilities

Intel Chipset Identification Utility
www.intel.com/support/chipsets/inf/chipsetid.htm

Sandra	www.sisoftware.co.uk
Ontrack JumperViewer	www.ontrack.com/jumperviewer

Audio technology

Dolby Labs	www.dolby.com
DTS	www.dtsonline.com
Steinberg	www.steinberg.net
THX	www.thx.com
DirectX	www.microsoft.com/windows/directx

Graphics technology

Nvidia	www.nvidia.com
ATI	www.ati.com
Matrox	www.matrox.com

CD/DVD technology

CD-Recordable FAQ	www.cdrfaq.org
DVD Demystified	www.dvddemystified.com
DVD+RW Alliance	www.dvdrw.com
DVD Forum	www.dvdforum.org

Hardware review sites

Tom's Hardware Guide	www.tomshardware.com
Motherboards.org	www.motherboards.org
ExtremeTech	www.extremetech.com
Anand Tech	www.anandtech.com
Digital-Daily	www.digital-daily.com

BIOS updates and information

Phoenix	www.phoenix.com
Award	www.unicore.com
AMI	www.megatrends.com
Bios-Drivers	www.bios-drivers.com

Manufacturers featured

Gigabyte	http://uk.giga-byte.com
AOpen	www.aopen.nl
Crucial Technology	www.crucial.com/uk/index.asp
Kingston technology	www.kingston.com/ukroot
Seagate	www.seagate.com
Mitsumi	www.mitsumi.de
Creative Labs	www.europe.creative.com
Lite-On	www.liteonit.com
Zalman	www.zalmanusa.com
Lian-Li	www.bossecomputers.com
US Robotics	www.usr-emea.com

Software featured

Windows XP	www.microsoft.com
Ghost	www.symantec.com

All you ever wanted to know about ...

Form factors	www.formfactors.org
Serial ATA	www.serialata.org
Wireless networking	www.wi-fi.org
PCI Express	www.pcisig.com

PART **6** # Appendix 5
Abbreviations & acronyms

A handy list of some shorthand terms used throughout
this manual or that you might otherwise encounter.

2D/3D	Two-dimensional/three-dimensional
2x/4x, etc.	Double-speed/quadruple-speed, etc.
A3D	Aureal 3D
AC '97	Audio Codec '97
AGP	Accelerate Graphics Port
AMR	Audio Modem Riser
ASIO	Audio Stream In/Out
ATA	Advanced Technology Attachment
ATAPI	Advanced Technology Attachment Packet Interface
ATX	Advanced Technology Extended
BIOS	Basic In/Out System
CD	Compact Disc
CD-DA	Compact Disc – Digital Audio
CD-R	Compact Disc – Recordable
CD-ROM	Compact Disc – Read-Only Memory
CD-RW	Compact Disc – Rewriteable
CMOS	Complementary Metal-Oxide Semiconductor
CNR	Communications and Networking Riser
CPU	Central Processing Unit
CRIMM	Continuity Rambus Inline Memory Module
DAE	Digital Audio Extraction
dB	Decibel
DDR-RAM	Double Data Rate – Random-Access Memory
DIMM	Dual Inline Memory Module
DMA	Direct Memory Access
DSL	Digital Subscriber Line
DTS	Digital Theatre Systems
DVD	Digital Versatile Disc
DVD-RAM	Digital Versatile Disc – Random-Access Memory
DVD-ROM	Digital Versatile Disc – Read-Only Memory
DVD-R/RW	Digital Versatile Disc – Recordable/Rewriteable
DVD+R/RW	Digital Versatile Disc – Recordable/Rewriteable
DVI	Digital Visual Interface
EAX	Environmental Audio Extensions
FAQ	Frequently Asked Questions
FAT	File Allocation Table
FSB	Front Side Bus
GB	Gigabyte
GPU	Graphics Processing Unit
HDD	Hard Disk Drive
HT	Hyper-Threading
I/O	Input/Output
ICH	Integrated Controller Hub
IDE	Integrated Drive Electronics
IEC	International Electrotechnical Commission
IEEE	Institute of Electrical and Electronic Engineers
ISA	Industry Standard Architecture
KB	Kilobyte
KHz	Kilohertz
LAN	Local Area Network
LED	Light-Emitting Diode
LGA	Land Grid Array
MB	Megabyte
Mbps	Megabits per second
MCH	Memory Controller Hub
MHz	Megahertz
MIDI	Musical Instrument Digital Interface
MP3	Motion Picture Experts Group Audio Layer Three
MPEG	Motion Picture Experts Group
NIC	Network Interface Card
NTFS	New Technology File System
Pentium 4	Pentium 4
PC	Personal Computer
PCI	Peripheral Component Interconnect
PDA	Personal Digital Assistant
PDF	Portable Document Format
PnP	Plug-and-Play
POST	Power On Self Test
PS/2	Personal System/2
PSU	Power Supply Unit
RAID	Redundant Array of Independent Disks
RAM	Random-Access Memory
RIMM	Rambus Inline Memory Module
S.M.A.R.T.	Self-Monitoring Analysis and Reporting Technology
SATA	Serial Advanced Technology Attachment
SCSI	Small Computer Systems Interface
SD-RAM	Synchronous Dynamic – Random-Access Memory
SPDIF	Sony/Philips Digital Interface
TFT	Thin Film Transistor
THX	Tomlinson Holman Experiment
UPS	Uninterruptible Power Supply
USB	Universal Serial Port
VGA	Video Graphics Array
Wi-Fi	Wireless Fidelity
ZIF	Zero Insertion Force

Index

Author	Kyle MacRae
Copy Editor	Shena Deuchars
Photography	Iain McLean
Front cover illustration	Digital Progression
Page build	James Robertson
Index	Nigel d'Auvergne
Project Manager	Louise McIntyre